Thinking of...

People-Centric
Process Management?

Ask the Smart Questions

By Mark McGregor & Ian Gotts

Smart Questions™ Philosophy

Smart Questions is built on 4 key pillars, which set it apart from other publishers:

1. *Smart people want Smart Questions not Dumb Answers*
2. *Making it easier for Domain experts to get into print*
3. *The community has a great deal to contribute to enhance the content*
4. *We donate a percentage of revenue to a charity voted for by the authors and community. It is great marketing, but it is also the right thing to do*

www.Smart-Questions.com

Reviews

This is a topic that is close to my heart. I am a firm believer in engaging the people in solving problems and improving what is done. In a world where process seems to mean technology, this book offers a timely reminder of the pivotal role that our people play in real success. We have made huge strides here over the last year particularly in changing the culture to one where staff are much more engaged in the work and continuously looking for ways to improve and to eliminate wasteful activities. We've seen tremendous results in terms of efficiencies and service improvements. I would strongly recommend this book to anyone looking to improve their capability in process improvement or looking to drive real results from process improvement programmes.

Maurice Chadwick, Operations Director, Bank of Ireland

Much of the literature on business process management coming from IT vendors and consulting firms is much to do about serving up answers. But because every company and every situation is unique isn't it time to ask questions first? McGregor and Gotts do just that and more; they provide the right questions that will guide you along the path to achieving meaningful business results from your process initiatives.

Peter Fingar, Former CIO, Professor and author

For those with an interest in process management, make this one of the first books you read. The book's central lesson – that deep interaction with people is essential to improve process performance – should not be forgotten. Although many analysts, vendors, and IT personnel enjoy discussing the range and sophistication of functionality in BPM technology, the authors remind us that all progress finally depends on human adoption. A process that uses a sharp stick to spear fish near shore is much more effective than a 60-foot fishing boat that cannot get out of dock for lack of a capable crew

Jim Boots, Senior BPM Adviser, Chevron

An insightful book about the central role that people play in any effective business process. Automating and measuring processes are important, but in the end, it always comes down to the managers and employees who have to do the work. This book will make sure you ask the right questions when you approach your next process project.

Paul Harmon, Executive Editor, BPTrends

This book, particularly the 'smart questions', reminds us that process management delivers value when people find, understand and adopt the processes in question. As a business process outsourcing provider we are custodians of the processes we deliver for our clients and our success in continuously improving the performance of these services depends on a people centric approach, with a transparent understanding of process and performance shared between service provider and client. It's a recipe for successful process improvement and long term client relations. If you have an interest in this field I'd recommend you take account of the people-centric questions before considering which business process technologies to choose.

Sean Murphy, Head of BPO Performance Improvement, Steria

Although some organizations have moved forward with BPM initiatives and seen significant success, there's still a large part of industry which sees BPM more as "yet another three-letter-IT-acronym" than as a business initiative with real value. This book helps to demystify how to get started with BPM and see it for what it can be at its best: a way for organizations to improve the process of process improvement – collaboratively driving change, sharing knowledge and empowering their workforces to participate in improvement.

Neil Ward-Dutton, Research Director, MWD Advisors

There are many books on Business Process Management, and its derivatives but few address the biggest challenge which is the People Side of Processes. It is written by two of the leading authorities in Business Process Management who are known for their depth of experience and their pragmatic approach to what is an increasingly important topic. It is a 'must read' for all leaders whatever the size, sector or maturity of their organisations.

Roger Cliffe, Quality Director, Vodafone Group Services

If you take a step back and look at any business process, can you imagine a business process without a person involved? No matter how much of the process is automated, at the end of the day there is always somewhere a person making use of that process. Think about it, the purpose of a business process is all about delivering value for somebody. So, the best way to look at a process is to look at the people involved. This book tells you where to look.

Frits Bussemaker, Korstmos & Founder BPM-Forum Netherlands

Technology was intended to aid human development, but its methodology gradually took on a prescriptive and restrictive role in this regard, tending to forget the people in the process. Mark and Ian through their work and this book "People-centric Process Management", lead the way in bringing us back to the point where we remember that it is people who manage technology and people who manage process. This book is invaluable for all of us, wherever we are and whatever approaches we use. Because the book is not intended to be yet another roadmap, but instead it leads us to ask the right, smart questions and to aid us and our organizations on their journey and to keep our eyes on the end users. Keeping the issues of all our people, teams, users, stakeholders and customers as a central theme.

Hardus Snow, CEO South African Development Foundation

It's a refreshing change to see a book solely concentrate on the 'business' side of Business Process Management and not only this, but the very People that make the organization run like clockwork whose opinion and input are often ignored during change. The book balances existing and new ideas side by side with some interesting case studies which the reader can instantly recognize and relate to within their own enterprise. The people-centric Smart Questions are thought provoking and guide the reader through the challenges of implementing process management, such as process governance, risk and controls, cultural change, whilst introducing new topics for consideration like Cloud BPM. Overall a good introduction to the human side of Business Process Management without the IT jargon.

Theo Priestley, Independent BPM Strategist and Analyst

Authors

Mark McGregor

Mark has worked in the IT Industry for over 30 years, he has held executive positions with a number of software vendors. Well known for his ability to help companies bridge the gap between business and IT, more recently he has focused helping business understand how to maximize the value of process programs, from both a people and systems perspective.

Mark has authored four books *In Search of BPM Excellence*, *Thrive! How to Succeed in The Age of The Customer*, *Winning With Enterprise Process Management* and *Extreme Competition*. The range and depth of his experience lead him to be sought after for speaking, advice and workshops by users, vendors, analysts and conference organizers.

mark@markmcgregor.com

Ian Gotts

Founder and CEO of Nimbus, which has been offering their business process management solution as an On-Premise and Cloud Computing offering to major corporations including Toyota, Chevron, Nestle, and HSBC Bank for the last 12 years.

With offices in 10 countries they have won numerous awards; RedHot 100, Gartner Cool Vendor in BPM, CIO.co.uk Top 20 companies to watch, and Microsoft Best Use of Technology.

He is author of four books, *Common Approach, Uncommon Results* and *Why Killer Products Don't Sell* and two *Thinking of...* books on Cloud Computing which makes him a sought after conference speaker.

ian@iangotts.com

Table of Contents

Acknowledgements

For me this book is the result of a 5 year journey. A journey into trying to understand more about what makes great companies great and why others despite all the best intentions and technology seem on occasions to fall a little short. Along that journey I have met with thousands of people, all of whom have helped to refine my thinking in various ways. My first thanks has to go to all those who have attended my seminars and training programs, for you have allowed me to share thoughts and test ideas, you also provided me with new insights and stories. In understanding better what makes the difference in business there is no substitute for spending time with the leadership, in this respect I owe a debt of gratitude to Kishore Biyani, CEO Future Group, R. Santhanam, Chairman Hindustan Motors, Karen Slabbert, MD Gallagher Estates, Roger Cliffe, Director Vodafone and Maurice Chadwick, Director Bank of Ireland – all of whom gave their valuable time to sit with me and share what had worked and what had not worked in their business.

As I learned more about the importance of people in change, it seemed only right to learn from the best in the personal change field and in this regard I would like to thank Dr Richard Bandler, John and Kathleen LaValle and Robert Dilts in particular, through their research, training, and patience in working through my questions, I believe I now understand more about motivation and personal change than I ever thought possible. The last group of people who shared their lessons and insights into human behavior with me are a number of very special people in India, HH Sri Sri Ravi Shankar, Sri Meher Chaitanyaji, Sri Bharati Tirtha Mahaswami , Sri Vijayendra Saraswathi, Kailash.C and my "brother" Sai Sridhar – you have all shared so much and given so much, I remember well my promise to each of you, that I will use the gifts you have given me in the best way possible, to help as many people as possible achieve their dreams and realize the happiness they seek.

Finally, I want to thank Ian Gotts. I have been talking about this book for so long, but not actually writing it. Ian without your prodding, pressure and support I may still only be talking about it today, so thank you.

Mark McGregor

Foreword

Success in improving performance requires the right mix of focus on people, process, and technology. This book emphasizes the central role of people in this respect. The authors remind us that this idea is not new – but it's an important one that merits reinforcement. There are some other ideas in this book that are also not new, yet are seldom practiced. These include; viewing the business from the "outside-in" or the customer's point of view, remembering that the single most important objective of process improvement and management is to improve organizational performance, and that the central role of technology is to enable operational performance. Mark McGregor and Ian Gotts also reinforce these not so novel, but extremely important ideas.

I have been working in the area of process management for nearly two decades. Far too many companies fail to involve the right people in the right way when they engage in process management – and are then astonished when they end up with sub-optimal results. Over the years, I have also seen a significant proliferation of improvement methods and tools; total quality management (TQM), business process improvement, reengineering, six sigma, lean, lean six sigma, and most recently business process management (BPM) – just to name a few. Each major improvement method emphasized in theory that we need to look beyond local efficiencies and examine the entire system of people and processes. In practice, this rarely happens. Instead, the pragmatists take over.

They use phrases like "don't boil the ocean." They argue for projects of small scope, largely defined within departmental boundaries and by so doing fail to take advantage of key opportunities that occur at cross-departmental hand-offs. They accept sub-optimal results in exchange for a scope where they can exercise control. They fail to pay sufficient attention to people.

Only about 30 to 40% of major improvement efforts achieve stated goals. Why do companies continue to struggle given the long history of process thinking? Change is hard and process improvement and management almost always involves significant change. There are probably more ways to fail than to succeed.

However, the pitfalls of a fragile case for change and putting methods before outcomes are two of the major culprits, and attention to people is a large part of the story in each case.

Every successful process based project relies on a compelling case for change that engages both the key members of the leadership team and motivates employees at several levels to collaborate in achieving a common cause. Executives, middle managers, and employees are people too. When there's a fragile case for change one or more of the following conditions exist; the overarching vision and the specific goals of the initiative are unclear, there is a lack of collaboration among the members of the leadership team, there is a lack of a compelling story as part of a solid communication program to engage middle managers and front line employees.

A compelling case for change is usually built on a foundation of either an imminent threat or a perceived major opportunity. The core message is either, let's join forces and change how we work to survive or let's join forces and change how we do things to prosper. In some instances, there is a real threat and in other situations, a story is woven to create a threat. The best test of a compelling the case for change is whether people become willing followers and whether they are motivated to act with urgency.

Executives, middle managers and front line employees all need to understand the point of change in the same way and also agree with it. That's why the case for change needs to tell a compelling story that speaks both to the head and the heart. This is where viewing operations from the customer's point of view becomes important.

Customers are people too, and they don't care how your company is structured or what technology you have chosen to deploy. They simply want what they ordered, when they asked for it, complete, error free, and a high level of responsiveness to their questions and complaints. By viewing the business from the customer's perspective, executives can gain insight into a new set of metrics that can assist them in re-framing performance and can craft stories that engage the work force. That's important because what motivates executives doesn't necessarily motivate employees.

Executives care about competitive position and competitive advantage. Employees care more about other factors such as; providing superior customer service, making a difference, and improving their own working environment.

The other major pitfall occurs when companies fall into the trap of putting "the how" (methods and tools) ahead of why and what. This occurs whenever a selected method of improving or transforming operations overshadows the desired outcomes for customers and shareholders. This can happen with any of the currently popular improvement methods and tools. In emphasizing one of these methods and tools, often with quasi religious zeal, subject matter experts get caught up in the selected method or tool and are often able to draw executives along with them, as executives have a fondness for jargon and do have a tendency to chase fads. These companies preach customer satisfaction but practice cost reduction. In their fervor, they often forget to look at the business from the customer's point of view – or the "outside-in". They don't involve all the right executives in the right way, and pay insufficient attention to how certain changes may affect the people who will have to make the new process work.

So all kinds of people; executives, middle managers, employees, customers, suppliers, matter enormously when it comes to achieving significant and sustainable success in process based improvement.

Technology matters too. In fact, as the authors argue, it is difficult to imagine any major improvement effort that does not rely on enabling technology. That requires bridging the age old IT-business divide, and deploying IT to serve the needs of the business such that IT systems help people do work how they want to work. This will only happen when IT people come to better understand the needs of the business and the needs of the end customer.

You will find this book to be thought provoking. Take the time to review the people, process, and technology questions in Chapters 8 through 10. Reviewing these questions, answering the ones that apply to you with candor, and formulating your own "smart questions" is hard work – but worthwhile indeed.

What you will get out of it will be directly related to what you put into it. The good news is that Mark McGregor and Ian Gotts have created some useful guidelines and a "smart question" template that can launch you on your own journey in getting better at process based improvement and management.

Andrew Spanyi

Andrew Spanyi's work in the area of process management is recognized internationally. He has written numerous articles and two books on process management - *More for Less: The Power of Process Management* and *Business Process Management is a Team Sport: Play It to Win!!*

For further details please visit *www.spanyi.com*

Who should read this book?

People like you and me

This book is not technical, nor was it ever intended to be. It is aimed squarely at those who see IT as a utility that should be consumed to serve the business. Not the reverse. People like you and me.

This book is intended to be a catalyst for action aimed at leaders of process change or transformation projects. They have such a wide range of job titles that this Chapter would be 20+ pages if I tried to list them all. So instead we have decided to show some of the types of project that BPM is relevant to.

Process Improvement

Perhaps you are looking maximize organizational performance, drive up quality and conformance and enable a more agile response to change. According to surveys, less than 20% of business activities are capable of automation. The remaining 80%+ remain manual processes, knowledge about which may be the most valuable intellectual asset which your organization possesses. How are you safeguarding and improving that knowledge?

Performance Management

Improving performance is a high priority for every senior executive. Many now realize that it is not enough just to identify and measure Key Performance Indicators (KPIs). Measuring KPIs helps identify under-performing business areas, but will not provide the means required to fix them. That's performance *reporting* not performance *management*.

Software Implementation

Behind every ERP & CRM implementation is the desire to drive business transformation. But change management is hard – as often said "The soft stuff is the hard stuff". And if done badly, you can be sure that user adoption and the resulting ROI will fail to meet target.

Corporate Governance, Risk and Compliance

Every organization faces a greater regulatory burden - for example. FSA regulations, Basel II, Sarbanes-Oxley, ISO 9000 and ISO 17799. Yet compliance in itself is seldom the end game. After all, a well run business will pass audits more easily, but more importantly, it enjoys greater efficiency, safety and compliance at lower cost; the real end game.

Lean and Six Sigma

Lean Six Sigma is a business improvement methodology which combines tools from Lean Manufacturing and Six Sigma. Lean focuses on speed and lower waste; Six Sigma focuses on quality. By combining the two, the desired result is better quality faster and is applicable to any organization type. Process Management is the bedrock on which to build such initiatives.

Outsourcing

Whether you are an outsourced service provider or a client looking to outsource, one thing is clear. You need end-to-end process visibility and governance. Process management will ensure that you have a collaborative framework for performance improvement rather than an abrasive client-vendor relationship driven around a set of SLAs that are set in stone.

Quality Management

The quest for Quality Management should start with a robust examination of your business processes. Take a holistic view of processes across your organization so you can provide a real-time, contextual view of all activities, related quality requirements, performance, resources, systems, documentation and activity ownership. Successful quality accreditation should then become a by-product.

How to use this book

This book is intended to be the catalyst for action. We hope that the ideas and examples inspire you to act. So, do whatever you need to do to make this book useful. Use Post-it notes, photocopy pages, scan pages, and write on it. Go to our website and email colleagues the e-book summary. Rip it apart, or read it quickly in one sitting. Whatever works for you. We hope this becomes your most dog-eared book.

Clever clogs – skip to the questions

Some of you have a good understanding of the BPM and have a pretty good grasp of the implications, benefits and risks. Therefore you have permission to skip to Chapter 7 where the structure of the questions is explained.

But before you go, please read "Getting Involved" on the next page. You can always come back to Chapters 1-5 later.

Getting Involved

The Smart Questions community

There may be questions that we should have asked but didn't. Or specific questions which may be relevant to your situation, but not everyone in general. Go to the website for the book and post the questions. You never know, they may make it into the next edition of the book. That is a key part of the Smart Questions Philosophy.

Send us your feedback

We love feedback. We prefer great reviews, but we'll accept anything that helps take the ideas further. We welcome your comments on this book.

We'd prefer email, as it's easy to answer and saves trees. If the ideas worked for you, we'd love to hear your success stories. Maybe we could turn them into 'Talking Heads'-style video or audio interviews on our website, so others can learn from you. That's one of the reasons why we wrote this book. So talk to us.

feedback@Smart-Questions.com

Got a book you need to write?

Maybe you are a domain expert with knowledge locked up inside you. You'd love to share it and there are people out there desperate for your insights. But you don't think you are an author and don't know where to start. Making it easy for you to write a book is part of the Smart Questions Philosophy.

Let us know about your book idea, and let's see if we can help you get your name in print.

potentialauthor@Smart-Questions.com

Chapter

Why People-Centric Process Management

If we can really understand the problem, the answer will come out of it, because the answer is not separate from the problem.

J. Krishnamurti (Philosopher, 1895 – 1986)

THE lights dim, the audience quietens in response - and you step towards the rostrum. It was an extraordinary honor for you, Richard James, an amateur conductor, 'mere' business CEO, to be invited to do a cameo with the Vienna Philharmonic.

It was a simple piece of course, an early Mozart piano concerto, featuring a young Chinese pianist. But snow at O'Hare had cancelled two days of flights – so there had been no time for any rehearsals at all. Gulp - you lift the white baton to gather the orchestra. It was now or never. Hell, this was more nerve-wracking than any investor presentation.

But, really, what could go wrong? You knew the piece intimately. You had even conducted it before. And the Vienna Philharmonic musicians were among the world's finest. So relax and enjoy.

It was the second bar when you realized something was awry. The orchestra was going faster than you'd ever imagined.

It came crashing into your head that they were using the revised October 1782 score, while you had the original September 1781 score in front of you. Never mind – maybe you could still get through this.

The orchestra built raggedly towards the entry of the soloist, their eyes looking at you in increasing bewilderment, wondering why your arms were off-beat.

You turned to introduce the pianist. She played from memory of course. It was half a bar later that you realized that she was performing Mozart's later revision of this work – his January 1783 score, which was much the same, except for the revised timpani line.

The music careered along, jumping and spluttering like a car with water in the tank. Maybe it was OK for an amateur – you might just make it to the end.

But not much can survive when the timpanist is confused. The cacophony grew. Only true grit could save the day. You waved and pummeled the air, and pulled them through into the final bar - and silence.

First one clap, then another, then spreading around the hall – until finally tumultuous applause. You bowed, amazed, and left the podium.

In the wings, you overheard a radio presenter gushing into his microphone: '…a stunning new interpretation of Mozart in the style of Philip Glass …'

A miraculous survival – again. But as you headed back for a final bow – and definitely no encore – your thoughts turned inexplicably to work.

How well are your teams performing? Is it that talented heroics are required because everyone has a slightly different or no view of the playbook? How much more profitable could your company be if their skills were harnessed and directed?

Didn't you just put that process improvement project on the backburner? Wasn't it aimed at getting consistent processes and documents delivered real-time to all staff.

Hey, you might even get the Europeans onto the same page, at last.

The pressure of change

With the phenomenal pressure on organizations to make changes and fast, it is inevitable that processes are increasingly seen as holding the key to success. The idea is of course not new. Right from the earliest days of the Industrial Revolution processes have been created, changed and improved. Today, it seems that any talk of process is almost inevitably linked to talk of technology and how technology is required in order to deliver changes.

In the Business Process Management (BPM) world, we are seeing all kinds of variants on how that technology can be applied. We have System Centric BPM, Document Centric BPM and Human Centric BPM to name but a few. However, it is our contention that the missing link in many of these is People. So much of the focus has been around technology, doing things to people or replacing people, when instead we need to be engaging with people and helping them achieve their goals better.

We are not alone in this belief.

"We believe regardless of the middleware stack that customers choose, their biggest challenges are going to be around the people, processes and technologies that will allow them to meet or exceed their business objectives of agility, performance, security, availability and change."

Kelly Emo, Senior Product Marketing Manager, HP Software

So here we see one of the world's largest vendors reminding us at one level that we need to stay focused on the business goals, while at the same time reminding us that process and technology without the people element is not enough.

Conversely, we are of the belief that simply taking a non-technology approach to process improvement is to ignore the vital role that technology plays in our everyday lives and the opportunities that it creates for our businesses.

When promoting the idea of People-Centric Process Management, it is not our intention to suggest that other ways are wrong or that a new category is needed. This would only muddy the water even more. Instead we argue that by coming at your process improvement or process management project from the personal angle will actually assist you in making changes more easily. It will lead to faster and more sustainable results and to help avoid many of the problems that are faced by people following the existing tried and tested approaches.

What we are suggesting is not new. We have never been fans of ignoring the past and chasing Silver Bullets. Instead we are taking a look at what organizations that have successfully made moves in the direction of being more process oriented and distilling the essence of what makes them different and then sharing this with you. We have no desire to make you or your company into something you are not. But we do believe that the ideas and experiences here can help your company be the best you can be.

Whatever your business, the chances are that the processes that you might want to work on, document, or communicate are currently carried out by people. These people are smart, they understand how to do their job, and in many cases know how to get round failings in the current processes or procedures. They as individuals have more knowledge about the process inside their head than any process diagram or model can ever hold. Even the best analysts will struggle to be able to understand the complete process better than they do. And, probably their managers struggle as much as the analysts! How many call centre managers regularly take to the phones and force themselves to work through the exact methods that their staff do? Not enough.

Engaging with real end users

So as a first stage we suggest that it is better to engage with the end users who actually do the work, rather than through business analysts who are proxies for the end users. This is something that many people do, although we have seen a tendency to move toward electronic communication or conference calls. We suggest that if the problem you are working on is important enough then a more human approach using live workshops is not expensive in the long run.

If we were to tell you that we have looked at how you work and decided that we know better than you do how it should be done, how would you feel? We suspect that your first reaction might be "who the heck do they think they are" or something similar. So the chances are you would not be very receptive to our ideas for change.

On the other hand, if we suggested that there might be ways of being more effective and asked for your opinion then you are likely to tell us. If we were to then drive out the improvements in a joint workshop we are likely to find that you would not only embrace the change, but possibly even thank us for it!

Your people who are doing the work know what works, what doesn't and how it can be improved, so let's build on that.

IT needs to change, not people

When it comes to implementing technology systems the most common complaint that many of us hear is that we seem to always have to change the way we work to suit the system. Very few technology systems seem to work the way that we do or enable us to work the way we want to. For years technologists have come up with reason after reason to justify why we need to change. We suggest that the balance is changing. If you wish to sell technology systems to business users you have to show how it supports the way that people want to work. As people become more aware of technology, they are also becoming more aware of the fact that systems can be changed and interfaces redesigned to suit their needs. This will certainly increase the pressure on IT people to understand intimately the roles and requirements of the consumers/users of the systems they are building.

IT is just a department within the business and like the other functional groups it is staffed and run by people. There are of course those who suggest IT folks would be more like people if they got out more! But we think that is very unfair and is something of a throwback to the early days of computing. Where they are right is that people in the technology field are likely to have schooled, studied and worked almost exclusively in the technology field and this gives them a very myopic view of the business world. How many of your IT people came up through the ranks of business before coming across to IT?

We are reminded of a client we used to deal with many years ago, a large financial institution in New York. One day our contact called to say that they were moving on and that we would need to deal with someone else. We thanked them, expressed our sympathy and then asked where they were going. The reply surprised us. They said that actually they had to move out of IT and back into line management in the business. It turns out that this company had a policy in place to ensure that all staff had to rotate out of specialist departments like IT, Sales and Marketing into core business units on a regular basis. The price of not doing so was to be ignored for all future promotions. The benefit of course was that when they rotated back they had new appreciation and understanding of what challenges the business faced. This is something that will have been copied by too few organizations over the years.

It reminds us that IT is not the only area that can become disconnected. The same can be true for almost any department in an organization. In our modern world it may be that our quest for specialization has gone way too far. Once upon a time an MBA was a cross functional qualification. It was a point in one's career and learning where the horizons were broadened so that people became capable general managers. Now it seems that even in MBA land we can stay within our specialist area.

People are everywhere

In summary we believe that by thinking of people – the people that do the work, the people that manage the work, the people who are undertaking the improvement projects and the people who are our customers - is the smartest way of ensuring our best chance of success.

The more we focus on people as people, learning better ways of listening, understanding and communicating with them, then the less chance we have of creating resistance to change and wondering why group A is not able to communicate clearly with group B.

We offer this as an alternative way of thinking about your projects, programs and businesses. To work out whether it applies to you then think about the following statement.

If what you are doing now is delivering everything you desire then keep doing it. If however what you are doing is not delivering all that you desire, then do ANYTHING else but that!

In Chapters 2, 3, 4 and 5 provides some insight into how you can increase your chances of success. As you read these Chapters you will notice that although we provide thoughts, ideas and experiences, we do not provide you with a prescriptive "How to". This is intentional as the whole purpose of a book like this is to help you to ask the right or Smart Questions. It is one enabler in assisting you to find your own path.

In Chapters 8, 9 and 10 we start to look at the questions you need to think about. In addition to the questions we provide some of the thinking behind those questions. You may not need to be able to answer all the questions, but at least knowing the questions may help you understand some of the potential gaps in your thinking.

Finally in Chapter 11 we wanted to share some stories of success with you. In these we hope you may find some inspiration that helps you identify ways that might work for you, ideas that could help you build businesses cases more easily, or simply the motivation that helps you realize that the time for change is now.

Chapter 2

The Business of Process Management

An organization's ability to learn, and translate that learning into action rapidly, is the ultimate competitive advantage.

Jack Welch (former GE CEO, 1935 -)

WHEN starting out on Process Management, there has been a great tendency to focus on methods and tools. We suggest that such a fixation is a mistake. Process Management is fundamentally about improving the  performance of an organization. This simple statement is very often forgotten in the rush to apply the latest or greatest technology. No technology however great, is of any value unless it is going to help improve our business achieve its stated goals and objectives. Sounds, simple and seems like a statement of the blinding obvious, but if it is then consider the following.

In our experience, over 60% of people undertaking process improvement projects in public companies do not know what the corporate objectives of their company are! An even higher percentage, perhaps as many as 80%, have not or do not read the annual reports that their company has on public record.

Without taking the time and making the effort to understand the overall business objectives, the real business performance gains from change and process projects can become something of a lottery.

Companies such as Toyota, General Electric, South West Airlines and FedEx are frequently touted as great examples of organizations that have and do use process effectively in order to deliver business results at levels far above their competition. In the case of Toyota (Lean) and GE (Six Sigma), many people set out to copy the approaches they used in order that they too can reap the rewards. But take a moment and ask what things these organizations have in common? We are sure that you will have many things on your list, but we hope that you will agree with the following; *Innovation, Teams, Creativity, People, Process and Customer Centricity.*

So you set out to emulate in some way the achievements of these great companies. However, what we actually find is that people take the approaches (Lean, Six Sigma, etc) and then use them to focus on; *Rules, Regulations, Policies, Procedures, Individuals and Tasks.* Small wonder that despite all the effort, the rewards do not seem to come!

If your objective is to learn from these organizations, then at one level focus on the things that they did e.g. People and Process, while at the same time doing it the way that they did it. They did not simply copy someone else's method, they created one of their own. These organizations took some ingredients out of a number of other methods, ideas and approaches and then created their own recipe for success. We suggest that in considering how best to implement a Process Management, you should consider doing the same. Remember also, that the approach they may be known for today, was not a one shot. In the case of GE they had tried and failed several times to get process thinking embedded into the organization, before taking those lessons of failure and wrapping them into their flavor of Six Sigma.

Something else that these organizations had in common was their focus on solving business problems. Each of them did not bring in the new techniques or practices of working until they had identified that they were not solving business problems the old way.

So if what you are doing is delivering all the results your business needs, then Process Management is not required. However if what you are doing is not delivering what you need, the best advice is – "Do anything else than what you are doing".

For the remainder of this Chapter we will consider some of the more common business drivers from a slightly different angle, which we think can increase the level of success of your process projects and thus contribute more positively to the performance of your organization.

Increasing revenue

Every business is looking to cut costs. But the best companies know that actually it is waste they want to cut, not cost. Of course the action to reduce costs may also be driven by poor or ineffective management. This may sound harsh, but allow us to explain. If we assume that the objective of business is to generate profit then we all know this is simply what is left after we deduct cost from revenue. Again, stating the obvious, we could of course leave costs alone and simply increase revenue! How many of your process and change projects are geared towards winning new customers? Increasing business from existing customers? Stemming customer attrition? These are all ways in which we can contribute positively to the top line of our business.

Experience shows that executives hear almost every day some new way of cutting costs, but rarely are they presented with new or novel ways of using what they have to help increase revenue. We also suggest that if you are trying to construct a business case for process management or change, it will be even more powerful if it links to increasing revenue.

As part of any business case you put forward you should consider adding a section that explains how the initiative can help to increase revenue. Enabling businesses to grow in a healthy way is vital if we are to create the vast numbers of jobs that are required to offset the troubles of the past few years.

Reducing waste

During and immediately following the Credit Crunch most organizations are having to find new ways of operating. For many this means looking to reduce costs. It seems that increasingly people are turning to Process Management as a way of reducing costs and trying to manage their way out of the situation. And for some this may well be the correct approach. The challenge will be how well apply it. Will they go with a sledgehammer to crack a nut, or will they look at the wider possibilities and allow themselves to position for success?

It will be fascinating to see whether we go for the history repeating approach or learn the lessons from the past. Those with long memories will remember that Business Process Reengineering (BPR) was seen as a tool to help businesses out of the earlier recession, then as business picked up people said that BPR did not work and was too blue sky. The lesson of course is that everyone was focused on removing cost as opposed to removing waste. It is the removal of waste that will serve us when the upturn in the market starts.

Now though, there is a need to chase efficiency and whilst true to form many will simply ask their purchasing people to squeeze their suppliers, we suggest that this is a lazy approach and is management acting without managing. Simply taking costs out of a business across the board has never been seen as a successful long term survival strategy in the past and there is no reason to believe it will be the right strategy for the future.

Instead managers should focus on getting a better handle on their cross functional or business processes and allowing their own staff to identify waste or non-value adding activities that can be eliminated. By removing waste, as opposed to cost, will mean that the company is not being damaged in any way and will in fact be in a better position to serve its customers in the market upturn. Some smart organizations may well realize that if they do this well, they may actually be able to go to their clients and offer cost reductions without being asked. This will forge stronger relationships and potentially even increase their market share. Now, wouldn't that be neat? Remove waste, leading to lower costs, which leads to higher revenues. Seems like a win-win.

Greater effectiveness

We know that we need to be efficient, but what if we are efficient without being effective?

The difference between the two is that efficiency tends to be an *inside out* perspective - what can we do to be more efficient (improve OUR processes, cut OUR costs, remove waste from OUR system). On the other hand effective is an *outside in* perspective. It does not matter what we want to do. What does matter is what the customer wants from us and how can we deliver it to them to the quality they seek at a price they are willing to pay. This causes us to do only the steps we need to and therefore eliminates unnecessary work and doing things that customers won't pay for.

A classic example here is the auto industry. Whether we consider the ailing US firms or the almost totally non-existent UK firm is of no consequence. In both cases in response to pressure from Asian car companies the US/UK manufacturers seemed to chase two things in particular. Quality and efficiency. They woke up to the fact that they needed to drastically improve their quality and efficiency, they tried (and are still trying) to become more efficient, producing their cars at lower costs. They have all to a greater or lesser degree made some major strides in both of these areas.

However, notwithstanding the current financial crisis, as Barack Obama suggested last year, the US car firms have still not made the changes they need to in order to give themselves a real shot at long term survival. Unlike their Asian counterparts they were too focused on efficiency and not enough on being effective. If we look at the world market for autos over the past 10-15 years we see that it is Japanese companies who have consistently delivered the products that customers wanted, not merely trying to find innovative ways of getting customers to buy what the manufacturers wanted to make!

Truly successful organizations in every sector have proven that understanding what the customer wants and will pay for is critical. To operate processes that deliver to these criteria makes sense. To then identify ways of ensuring that the required activities are executed efficiently is obvious. It is these things when taken together that means we are and can be effective and makes our processes world class. To do anything less is to waste time, money and other resources and to risk the entire health of the enterprise.

By way of an example of how "efficiency" by itself can be misleading, consider the following quote:

RBS was a slightly odd organization in those days. In many ways, it appeared remarkably successful. Having acquired NatWest and expanded massively in the US, it was one of the world's biggest and most profitable banks. But it was always rather secretive and surprisingly defensive: I'm struggling to remember a single on-the-record interview given by Goodwin to a broadcaster or newspaper. It was more inward looking than most huge international companies, and was very prickly about even mild criticism. That said, many in the City, and many journalists, admired the bank for its efficiency and Goodwin for his "Fred-the-shred" moniker - his reputation as perhaps the most fearsome and effective cost-cutter in UK corporate life. So it's striking that the new chief executive, Stephen Hester, has identified some £1.5bn to £2bn of cost savings at the bank, which are apparently above and beyond what has already been disclosed. And Hester will announce as much this Thursday.

Robert Peston, BBC Business Editor in Feb 2009

Here Peston is talking about a company that was seen as successful as measured by its industry peers and its apparent efficiency. The key points being that it was defensive, unwilling to accept criticism and inwardly focused. How many organizations can we think of that these terms could apply to?

Had they been more focused on being *effective* they would have able to learn from criticism, been more focused on the needs of their customers, constantly questioning whether there were better ways of doing things and looking at business in a more cross functional way. Given the problems in the whole financial sector, it would be naive to suggest that these things alone would have prevented failure. Of particular note though is the fact that even one of the most apparently efficient organizations in their industry can mysteriously find such amazing amounts of additional savings when push comes to shove.

Being effective, still enables us to gain from efficiency, it just enables us to ensure that we are focused on ensuring that we are doing what we actually need in order to survive and thrive in business.

Enhancing customer service

However we look at it, most businesses can and will only survive by delivering on service excellence. We can call it by any name we like, but the fact is simple, if we do not deliver products or services that delight the customer, someone else will and we will lose customers.

The customer is King, he can fire everyone in the organization from the CEO down – simply by spending his money elsewhere

Wal-Mart founder Sam Walton

Process Management offers some great opportunities to enable us to take our customer service to a whole new level. Unfortunately, to date many organizations are using the label of service to simply force customers into either interacting in new ways or pushing work out of their organization and on to the customers. This approach is not so much about delivering quality customer service as it is about removing cost from our business.

Our experience suggests that when considering processes one should start with the customer. It is amazing what you can find when you simply ask what an activity or process is doing to contribute to the desired result the customer requires. The chaotic way in which our organizations have evolved usually means that we have many rules, policies and procedures being in place for historical rather than current business reasons.

Of course, these customer centric processes also enable us to focus on what it is we actually do and need to do, rather than what we want to do.

Focusing on customer service is vital for many reasons. Surprisingly enough, happy customers stay with us longer and spend more money thus increasing revenues. Processes that focus on the customer tend to be more effective, thereby eliminating much waste.

Most process improvement programs focus on cost reduction or increased efficiency. But think for a moment about how much better your business might be if instead it focused on waste reduction, increased effectiveness, better customer service and increasing revenue.

The idea is not for everyone, but we are certain that if we were to look back we would see that the truly great companies have not been content to simply find new ways of doing old things. They will have focused on doing new things in new and innovative ways. Always willing to use the lessons of the past, but blending it with the shiny and new.

If you do think that perhaps changing your thinking and coming at things from a different perspective is right for you, then the discussions in the next few Chapters will help you to consider ways to supplement the approaches you already use.

Retain the culture, rewrite the rules

Kishore Biyani, Managing Director, Pantaloon Retail

Chapter

The Process of Change

It is change, continuing change, inevitable change that is the dominant factor in society today. No sensible decision can be made any longer without taking into account not only the world as it is, but the world as it will be.

Isaac Asimov (Author, 1920 - 1992)

IF you talk to people about how they go about understanding and improving processes, pretty quickly the discussion descends into a debate around methods and tools. We soon find ourselves discussing the relative merits of BPM vs. Lean Sigma vs. Six Sigma, of EFQM vs. AQPC, which modeling tool to use or which BPM vendor to talk to.

Very soon people are talking about how they are going to analyze processes and problems and how they are going to improve or automate them. Keep talking and listening and eventually two things will come up. Firstly, there will be a discussion around how the method or technique needs to be applied but how they don't have the budget for training, and secondly that they know how to do it but people are simply not buying into the change. Of course other issues such as communication and lack of management support are also factors, but in some ways these also relate to the issue of change.

We have found it fascinating over the years just how few people or organizations have in place or have even studied the "Process of Change." If change is so important to us and is such an ongoing thing, then why does every organization not have a well documented and well exercised process for change? Why do people not understand that effective change begins not by analyzing the problem, but instead by elaborating the opportunity and eventual goals and aims? Perhaps it is something to do with the lack of breadth of our studies or perhaps it is because the people we rely on to do the work are analysts and naturally they are good at analyzing problems.

To the man with a hammer everything looks like a nail

Mark Twain

The same struggle also takes place in the field of personal change. On one side we have old school traditional therapists for whom the analytical approach is the one upon which they rely. On the other hand we have the newer breed of people who practice more holistic ways of helping people, and they are proving that Neuro Linguistic Programming (NLP) is a major step forward.

Just as with IT and process change, the starting point for the old-school is to analyze what exists and to ensure that this fully understood. Only then to do they lead people in a new direction. For practitioners of a more holistic approach, the best way is to light up the destination first and then simply to show people how to get there. It seems that this can in many cases be faster and certainly appears less painful. The key to this approach is a deep understanding of the process of change.

There are always new ways of doing things. The old is not bad, just old. New does not have to be good, just new.

The art is to blend what works from the old with what works from the new and that delivers the best results in the shortest practical time with the least possible pain.

In order to be better able to consider new ways of working we would suggest that perhaps some in the process community might benefit from studying more widely. Process, like so many disciplines today, seems to suffer as a result of "in-reading".

By way of a change the following might assist in generating new ideas or new trains of thought; Daniel Pink's *A Whole New Mind*, Malcolm Gladwell's *Blink*, Robert Cialdini's *Influence: The Psychology of Persuasion* and Marcus Buckingham's *First Break all the Rules*. All of these address the area of change, which is what we are about, but from different angles.

We especially recommend any books on the areas of creativity, innovation and communication as these will help focus our minds on solutions rather than problems.

Understand the Phases of Change

It is one thing to understand how the cycle of change works in order to effect change. However it is another to know when to apply it. Some years ago Dr Cynthia Scott and Dr Dennis Jaffe created what is known as the Scott and Jaffe Change Curve. They identified that there were four stages of transition; these are Denial, Resistance, Exploration and Commitment. We have reproduced a version of the curve below.

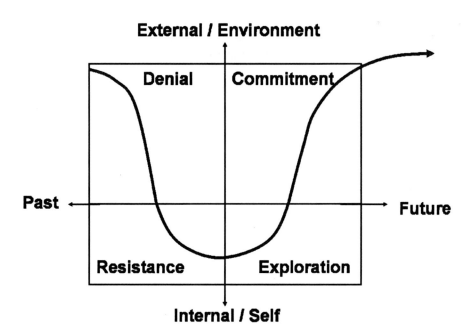

It is suggested, and supported by a large body of research, that when any of us is faced with change that these are the stages we go through. In addition it should be noted that when in **Denial** we are very much thinking about the past and the external environment – " They can't do this, everything was going great" as we move to **Resistance** we are still thinking about the past, but now about ourselves too – "I liked things the way they were", then as we go through to **Exploration** we are still thinking about ourselves, but now we are thinking of the future "I'll never be any good at this" or "I can't imagine enjoying that", finally as we move to **Commitment** we remain focused on the future, but once again think outside ourselves – "This will be better for the planet" or "The team needs to change to be successful"

Depending on the individual's personality and the magnitude of that individual's perceived loss, reaching the **Exploration** and **Commitment** stages can be difficult for both the individual and the organization in which he or she works. We should also remember that we are all going through the curve all the time and may be at different stages at the same time. We could be denying change with our partner, resisting change with our children, while exploring changes with a social group and actually be committed to changes at work and many other things concurrently.

Understanding this multiple position mindset is vital for us in process improvement, for we need to be applying the right strategy to help people. Very often when someone is seen as being negative we assume it is about changes at work, when in fact they could be exhibiting negative behavior as a result of other changes in their lives.

Of all the stages, when it comes to changing the way that people work, the **Exploration** phase is the key one. Trying to get people to change will not work until they are at the point of **Exploration.** It is when people are exploring that you will it best to use the cycle of change described above.

Rather than focus on which quadrant we can simply think about whether people are worrying about the past or the future and whether they are thinking of themselves or others.

This can more often than not be gleaned just from listening to the language they use to discuss the situation. Our advice, if they are talking about themselves, then you need to talk about the change in respect to them, if they are talking about the past then you must ensure that you too talk to the past. Only once you have joined their *world* can you try to lead them to yours.

It is exactly this leading people from one world to the next that the cycle of change is designed for. It does offer some ideas on short circuiting the system and if you want to know how to do it, it is simple, just ensure that the future is powerful and compelling. Be aware though that compelling for you does not mean compelling for them.

The following suggestion may not work for everybody all the time so we suggest that you take care. If we accept that the only time when people are going to listen to ideas or consider new ways of working is when they are ready to explore then helping them to get through denial and resistance as soon as possible can be an advantage. To this extent we need to get them to a point of accepting that the future is going to be different and that there is no point in resisting the change. It sounds very much like tough love, which it can be. But, it can just as easily be accomplished by involving the team in the changes earlier e.g. if we get them involved at the problem identification stage. In fact our experience shows that if we get teams involved at this stage they move to exploration and acceptance far quicker than many of the managers they work for.

Some of the things that you can do to help people through are:

- Ensure that they understand why there is a need for change and that the reasons behind it are good - which means good in their mind.
- Take a chance, bring in those most likely to resist at the earliest opportunity and listen to them and talk to their fears. Remember if they are in the Resistance box they won't care about others, they will care about themselves.
- Provide training, both to relieve the stress of change, as well as learning new skills. This will naturally cause them to do some exploring.
- Gradually ensure that the old way of working disappears, it is hard to go back to something that does not exist.
- Be supportive, acknowledge and reward the accomplishments and the sacrifices people have made.

Perhaps the most important thing though is work hard on the communication. Communication needs to be of the appropriate type and at the appropriate frequency - too much and it is ignored, too little and people feel ignored. A final recommendation on communication is to make more use of face to face communication. If you rely too heavily on electronic forms of communication you are increasing your chances of failure

We can't solve problems by using the same kind of thinking we used when we created them

Albert Einstein (Scientist 1879-1955)

Looking outside business for inspiration

While process improvement and change projects have been going on for many years, it seem that to date results have been mixed and no particular approach has dominated. So the question then was in what other field have people been more successful in creating lasting changes? This of course led to the fields of personal development and change and in particular NLP.

A part of the original thinking in NLP was that if we could find a way to codify how great people achieved the results they did, then we could find ways of learning those patterns and teaching them to others. This appeared so similar to what many were seeking to achieve through process improvement that we decided to research it further. Following on from detailed research and coming up with a theory, it seemed only right to test that theory with the creator of NLP – Dr Richard Bandler. So it was that some years ago on a cool autumn day in Edinburgh the opportunity presented itself for Mark.

The following is an extract from that conversation, which ties in with the Effective Change Strategy circle.

"When you help someone you first seem to focus on ***discovering*** what it is that somebody wants, have them describe their compelling vision of the future or positive view on why their life will be better. Then you have them go into detail on this in such a way as to have them really associate with it. During this you listen very carefully for clues and challenge them so as to ensure that they really do want to make changes and test for the level of seriousness.

Once you are satisfied you appear to move on to the next step. This is when you start to ***analyze***, to ask questions of them to understand more about what might be stopping them achieving the results they desire. Also, to think about which of the tools, techniques or patterns might be the most appropriate to achieve the results they are looking for.

Once you are happy that you understand what they want and how you might help them you ***design*** an approach or intervention to achieve the desired result. Before actually performing any change work, you then check in with them to ***validate*** that they are totally happy to make the changes and will be comfortable with the results, only when you are sure that you have total agreement do you move on.

If you don't have full agreement, you appear to go back to the first step and once again try to ***rediscover, analyze*** and ***design*** before once again trying to ***validate***.

Now, with their full agreement you undertake the change work, you *implement* the changes with them and lead them to the point where they are learning new habits, behaviors and changes for themselves, you are providing them with new choices and helping them get a different perspective on things.

Once they have come to their own realization, or had their own 'aha' moment, you help them to *integrate* those learnings. Help them generalize the learning out into other areas of their life, areas where they believe that the new choices will serve them better. Having integrated the change, you provide them with techniques to ensure that they can hold on to the gains they have made to *manage* the changes and themselves.

Finally, you have them look at other areas of their life where the new perspective can serve them better, to have them generalize and *improve* those things that will serve them more usefully in the future."

So, if this appears to be the process which one of the most successful personal change agents of our time uses, and the one on which most other successful personal change personalities have based their own work and businesses, then why is it that we seem to try and avoid using the same process in our business?

What is different from the personal and the business driven changes? The process of change is universal and the above can easily be adapted to business and process problems. The longer we try to avoid such a process then surely the longer we are going to take to successfully embed a culture of change within our organizations.

The difference is that in business we often discover and analyze the past – the Current State (As-Is) – rather than paint a compelling picture of the future – the Future State (To-Be).

The question is, where will you look to enhance your understanding of the process of change? How can taking a different perspective enable you to be even more effective than you are now?

What motivates change?

By now, you've probably realized that change is not one-size-fits-all. Every organization, based on its culture, maturity and market conditions will need to address change in a different way to ensure that the desired results are achieved. The type of change can be analyzed by considering three different factors.

Speed. How important is speed to accomplishing the objectives of the change effort? Is the pace determined by the markets, the competition or the customers?

Conformance. How closely must we follow the specific processes or outcome to achieve our goals? Is there regulatory pressure to conform or would it stifle innovation?

Commitment. How important is it to ensure that everyone in the negotiation understands the need for change and is prepared to do what it takes?

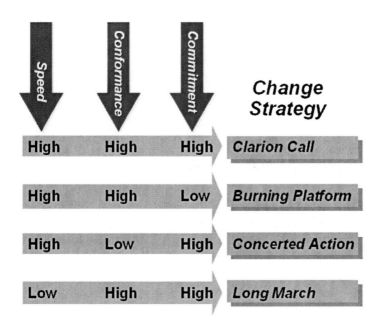

Speed	Conformance	Commitment	Change Strategy
High	High	High	Clarion Call
High	High	Low	Burning Platform
High	Low	High	Concerted Action
Low	High	High	Long March

If you then consider the relative importance of each of these three factors together, you identify the most appropriate change strategy, as we have shown in the diagram.

Clarion call: Requires that the change is driven by senior management leadership who show a strong commitment to the change. This is because the need and speed for change are not apparent further down the organization.

Burning platform: Everyone already recognizes the need for change. Therefore a clear message about what is required to change is needed. The risk is that the actions from different parts of the organization (in their panic) are uncoordinated and inconsistent.

Concerted action: This requires delegation of the change so that it can be applied autonomously throughout the organization. Yet it still requires the changes to fit within the overall business strategy.

Long march: A long-term initiative which has a strong identity and clear sponsorship from the top so that there is continued commitment to the change. No-one loses sight of the end goal. It also requires clear metrics to show that the changes are working.

Each strategy has its own attributes, but all of them require a consistent communication of what is required both down and across the organization. Clearly the urgency and tone of that communication varies.

What is common in these strategies is the need for every part of the organization to have a shared understanding of what is required of them. The communication that is required is not a 'weekly email from the CEO'. The communication needs to cover who needs to change, what behaviors need to change, what day-to-day activities will be different, what organizational or reporting structures have changed, and what physical changes need to happen. But to be able to get adoption and buy-in to the change, that communication also needs to put into the context of why the change is needed, and the expected results of the change – i.e. why it will be better.

Chapter

The Wisdom of Crowds

When I get ready to talk to people, I spend two thirds of the time thinking what they want to hear and one third thinking about what I want to say.

Abraham Lincoln (American President, 1809- 65)

A commonly heard phrase amongst executives today is "people are our biggest asset". The question is, if this is true then why don't people feel like it? Why don't they feel rewarded, empowered and valued?

If you don't really care about your people, then why should they care about you, or your customers?

Successful process management initiatives will need to address this issue head on if they are to deliver on their promise. It is no use hiding behind technology or trying to automate people out of your company. The fact remains that for most organizations "People Performing Processes Produce Profit" – so ignore the people and you can effectively ignore the profit too!

More than this though, it is your people who have the knowledge that is key to your being able to unlock the business benefits we talked of in Chapter 1. As many organizations have already found, to simply automate the discovery of process merely enables one to build new ways of doing old things, for many it also means building in waste and poor practice into shiny new systems.

There are those who suggest that this is why they employ analysts to look at the situation, but it is our contention that the role of the analyst is to facilitate the process not to drive it. Few of us like the idea of being told that what we are doing is wrong or hearing a so called "smart-ass" tell us they know better. However, most of us if asked would happily suggest new or better ways of delivering our work, if engaged or facilitated effectively.

The idea that the knowledge of the group is worth more than the sum of the parts is the subject for James Sorowicki's book *The Wisdom of Crowds*. In it he lists countless examples where the power of the group thinking was better than even the smartest of the so called experts. This is what we suggest we need to bring to bear in our efforts to improve. This is core to the success of companies like General Electric, Toyota, and South West Airlines. They have learned how to embrace and harness the knowledge of all their people and to leverage the sum of that knowledge for the good of their customers and their businesses.

In order that we too can leverage this knowledge we will need to learn to practice the 3 E's – Engage, Educate and Empower.

Engage: we need to better engage with our people, to make them feel valued and to make them understand how their contribution to change is vital for our long term success.

Educate: we need to invest in them, to provide education and training in order that they can make the best contributions that they can. This does not have to involve weeks or even days of training, but can be done via lunch brown-bags or other short sessions. As a word of caution we suggest that you do not rely on electronic training here. We are looking to engage and educate at an emotional level and this is best done with people physically present.

Empower: we need to empower people to make decisions and to be willing to act on their instincts. They also need the space and forgiveness to make mistakes. The phrase empowerment has been fashionable over the past few years and many shy away from it, especially in command and control organizations, but it really is vital if you want to get the most from people.

As an aside, remember years ago if you had a problem with a hotel you had to speak with a manager to get a resolution. Now the problem is usually resolved by the staff on reception. Initially the idea of empowering reception staff to change bills or give away free nights was met with horror. Now management understands that actually as customers we will accept a lesser compensation, if delivered in a timely manner. Staff know that it is not good to give away everything, so in reality hotels are giving away less for poor service, but we as customers feel better treated on the whole.

It is one thing to look to involve as many people as possible in your programs or initiatives, but different groups have different perspectives and if we are to be successful we need to take account of all of these.

Different strokes for different folks

Processes are clearly critical to the running of an operation so it is important that all the groups involved have a consistent and aligned view of how the business operates. Some of the key groups from a process perspective would be the End Users or Business Users, IT Department, IT Vendors and Risk/Compliance Managers. Our lives would be so easy if all these stakeholders were able to collaborate over a single source of the truth as regards to process.

One way to achieve this is to have one integrated process model, which includes all of their requirements. However, will this ever be possible? A short conversation with each of them will quickly reveal that their interpretations of what is a process and what should be in a process model and how they would use it are quite divergent.

What we do know however is that when individuals representing all of the above groups in a workshop scenario, they can quickly create maps of processes and identify opportunities for improvements.

One client we worked with held a 2 day workshop to identify and improve one of their end to end processes. They saved over £1million. We are not talking about a long winded improvement implementation here, but the savings were made before the workshop had even finished. It turns out that none of the participants had ever understood the end to end process, but as soon as they had captured it together, they collectively identified numerous "silly" things that the company was doing that could simply be stopped. As it happens they also identified many other improvements that could be made and the company went on to save many more millions as a result.

Of course this approach did not rely on or make use of technology; but simply involved getting a group of stakeholders together and leveraging the collective wisdom of the crowd. This approach to process and business improvement is not new. It is in fact a variant on the "Work Out" system pioneered by General Electric. Despite all the advances made by GE with Six Sigma, they still credit "Work Out" as being the technique that has done most to ensure that they are able to keep waste out of their systems and to improve the products and services they offer.

A key learning point from both our own workshops and the system used by GE is that it involves management getting out of the way. Let the people who have the suggestions implement them and you will find that the resistance to change will simply melt away. The role of managers is purely to lead, guide and coach the teams into identifying and making changes for themselves.

We find that when individuals representing these different groups discuss processes, they seem to naturally assume that the others in the conversation have exactly the same understanding or the term *process*. When in reality they usually all have a different view. Everyone leaves the meeting thinking that they are in complete agreement, but then are horribly confused when they act differently.

What hat do you wear?

One way that we have found to consider the different perspectives is to use hats. We understand that each of the four groups has in most cases valuable inputs and concerns about any given process. At the same time we also find that it is important to differentiate between the differing views and perspectives. Using the hat system described below in workshop situations has meant it is easier for people to appreciate other views, easier to build consensus and easier for people to identify risks and priorities. The following is a simplified take on what each hat represents and the key needs of each group represented by the hat color and style.

End Users

End users (or business users) are focused on delivering business results through processes. They understand that processes are how they work and deliver the products or services that provide value to our customers. These people also understand that good internal processes assist with staff training and ensure consistency. For some business users good processes also make it easier to move staff around or to expand operations, they use them to enable scalability. They are interested in ensuring that processes are logical, effective and accessible – in short they want processes that help them work the way they need to, they do not want to have to change the way they work to suit a new system.

These people understand the problems in the business and the frustrations of their customers. They are the source of a massive amount of knowledge.

On the down side they can also be blinkered at times into only seeing solutions from a very narrow angle, they can be the type of people that Henry Ford was thinking about when he said "If I had asked them they would have asked for a faster horse!"

These **End Users** we refer to as our **Green Hats**.

IT Department

The IT department wants to understand the business users' view of the operation to ensure that the IT systems they build and maintain truly support the business users, at minimum cost. They want to ensure that there is integrity of information as it flows around the systems. Paradoxically although they suggest that they are very interested in process, they are in fact interested really in procedure because it is at this level the software applications operate. The reasons being that in order to build a system one has to know exactly how a decision is made and which path to go down when, there is no room for ambiguity?

Traditionally IT departments have not had a great track record in understanding the business or the real needs of customers, but happily this is now starting to change. Conversely though because of technology there are new and innovative ways of doing business that many of our Green Hats could never dream of. So ensuring we that we are getting great advice from the IT department is vital, to ignore them is highly risky in today's world.

The *IT Department* is staffed with the **White Hats**.

IT Vendors

The IT system providers such as ERP, BPMS or Cloud vendors want to ensure that the configuration of their system is managed accurately and that it hangs together end-to-end i.e. passes System Testing and User Acceptance Testing. In short, they are looking to ensure that it meets the user needs, but more importantly perhaps that they can get paid quickly. Of course they do also want to ensure that they have happy and referenceable customers.

Although they talk to solving business problems and so try to align themselves with the Green Hats, they frequently find themselves as having more in common with our White Hats.

In an ever changing landscape they find themselves having to increasingly act like chameleons, on one hand they know that the Green Hats control the budget for them, while on the other hand the White Hats control the ability for them to be installed.

Good clear processes will usually lead to clear requirements from customers, thus making it easier for this group to identify how well suited their application or platform might be to the client's needs.

The danger with this group is that they have a tendency to always believe that their system does everything that everyone else does but better. This can make it hard for Green and White Hats to chose between Blue Hats.

The *IT Vendors* are **Blue Hats**.

Risk and Compliance

The Risk and Compliance Officers want to be able to demonstrate to auditors that end users are following a documented process, and that the correct risk control points have been identified and are effectively managed from a governance, ownership and auditing standpoint. Unfortunately in an ever regulated and litigious society the needs put upon business by risk and compliance is getting ever greater. This burden seems to fly in the face of waste removal or Lean initiatives, but does not look like getting better in the near future. So the risk and compliance team have a vital part to play in identifying, managing and improving processes.

The prime interest then is that of auditability and provability, some suggest that in simple terms their role is to keep management and executives out of jail. Whilst this may seem glib or trite it may be nearer to the truth than some people realize.

As with the other groups, they will look at the problem from their own perspective. The risk of course being that the cost of being compliant far outweighs the commercial benefit of compliance, as ever it is a balancing act.

This is the **Red Hat** perspective.

The more widely you are able to consult within your organization then the more involved people will feel, the more involved they feel then the more involved they will get. They, just like us at a fundamental level what to know WIIFM - What's In It For Me.

So the next time you think that you are in violent agreement - step back, look up and take a look at the hat the other person is wearing.

As we shall see in the next Chapter, understanding the different perspectives is vital when looking at the requirements of a BPM system.

Chapter 5

Dealing with the IT Dilemma

One machine can do the work of fifty ordinary men. No machine can do the work of one extraordinary man.

Elbert Hubbard (American writer, 1859-1915)

ALL organizations today are highly complex and trying to manage that complexity without the use of technology is practically impossible. Even the smallest organizations are dealing with a mass of legislative and regulatory requirements, if only in the areas of reporting, human resources and health and safety.

One of the key questions, in respect of Process Management, becomes whose project is it? Is it simply an IT project that we hand off to the technology folks to deal with or is it a business project that requires IT support? The answer to this may be simple – it is a business-led project - but it seems to have been made more complex than it may need to be.

For many organizations projects with a technology component are run and managed by IT with varying degrees of line of business involvement. Process improvement projects tend to fall into this camp. Part of the challenge for those taking an IT-led approach is rooted in history. There are few organizations where IT has a track record of delivering IT projects on time and within budget.

Our experience suggests that this tends to lead to a *done to* approach with the resultant resistance to change and potential business conflict.

The more successful approach seems to be where people run it as a business project that is aided and assisted by IT. This we see more as a *done with* approach and in these cases we see much less resistance and a greater cooperation.

Who has the problem?

The first part of our IT dilemma is what problem are you solving, and for whom? We have discussed in earlier Chapters how in effect all problems are business problems that can be aided or assisted by IT. We have said for some problems, technology offers us alternatives we might never have considered. However critical IT might be to a project it can never be thought of as an IT project. The only exception is where IT is in fact operating as a business unit. That is, the project is the improvement of the IT business – such as Service Delivery, Help Desk or Software Development.

If there are no IT projects only business projects, then projects can and should only start when a line of business manager identifies a point of pain and asks for assistance in dealing with it. From ITs perspective this last sentence makes life so much easier. By recognizing that projects are initiated by business users, IT does not need to worry about running round the business with solutions looking for problems; the cause of so much friction.

The business manager however also needs to remember that it is his pain and so simply throwing it over the fence to IT is not clever. If the project fails, ultimately it is he who will still suffer the pain. The business side needs to not only provide the budget but also make the people available too.

Level of IT support and involvement

Second then is to decide on what level of involvement your IT group will have in your chosen project, program or initiative. As we have said it is highly desirable to have some level of involvement.

For many organizations using techniques such as Six Sigma or Lean approaches they do not worry about this, we suggest that such organizations may be missing a trick and indeed risking duplicate work. There are many Lean and Six Sigma practitioners who use tools for statistical analysis but avoid using tools for capturing process flows, or possibly use very simple tools. This can lead to the "working" documents being lost at the end of the project.

We understand that such projects rarely provide full process documentation, but given that the process has to be understood to be improved, it makes sense to capture this information in a structured manner. Otherwise another group will have to duplicate the effort in order that they can make use of the process information. Better then to have people from your IT group involved in the first place, they can help to provide tools so that processes can be stored for later reuse and be communicated to the business.

But be wary. The IT department has a (White Hat) view of what a process is and therefore will try and provide tools to satisfy their perception of the requirements, not your real needs.

Process maps and content do not exist in isolation and being able to store them in a way that enables cross referencing, easy updating and later impact analysis requires that they are created and stored in a standardized way. By standardized we mean a way in which all maps within your company use the same symbols etc and are appropriately leveled.

You will also need the support of your IT group to help you work out the smartest ways of publishing the information in a secure and scalable way so that the content is available and useable by all who need access to it.

Who, when, how

Of course to capture, analyze and publish process information requires the use of BPM tools. We suggest that you need to think carefully about your objectives before selecting your tools in terms of Content, Presentation and Personalization.

Content: what information is stored – process diagrams, procedures, business rules, documents, links to application, metrics…

Presentation: what formats are required by the different audiences – process diagrams, XML, swimlanes, guided walkthroughs. And on what devices - PC, browser, mobile device, phone, tablet…

Personalization: who needs to be given easy access – access rights, search tags, custom intranet pages…

As an example if you intend to make the information about processes, procedures and measurements available as an on-line operations manual then you need to be careful in selecting your tool.

Many process automation tools (sometimes called BPMS) have some modeling capability and talk about publishing models, but very few are capable of delivering your content in a governed and appealing way, assuming that you want the information easily useable by end users. Their focus can often be the speed of automation without pausing to simplify the business operation first.

Another area to be wary of is the area of modeling, for many people the perceived cost of professional modeling tools is too high and instead they prefer to user lighter weight drawing, mapping tools or office packages. While these can look cheap initially they may actually work out more expensive in the end. The risk with these tools is that they do not enforce common ways of working and it is very difficult to relate one diagram to another and they have no centralized repository. This can lead to problems when looking at impact analysis, the naming of objects and governance.

Simulation and automation

Two other key areas to think about when selecting your tools are simulation and automation. Simulation is very often ignored or overlooked, in part because it is thought of as difficult and in part because it is an area that is very misunderstood. Most good modeling tools will provide you with some simulation ability. Even if you are not thinking of using it yet you should make sure that the tools you choose have the capability as you may need it for process optimization later.

With regard to automation, there are many different options. At the beginning of the book we talked about the fact that there are different types of BPMS platforms – Human-Centric, Workflow-Centric and Document-Centric to name but three.

It is important that you consider which type of problem you are trying to address before deciding which vendors to look at. This will take work on your part as many vendors will claim to be brilliant at all types, although they rarely are. A BPMS software application is only one option, but you may already have the capabilities in-house already

Take a look inside

Many organizations are now using ERP or some sort of packaged systems approach to IT in their business. Each of these can be thought of (with a Blue Hat on) as collections of processes delivered via a single product. While they have not been marketed in the past as process platforms, we will increasingly see them adapted for this market. Already one or two key vendors are specifically adding greater process platform capability. The question for you if you are using one of these already is whether the best solution to your problem might be a simple reconfiguring your existing ERP package or possibly even providing the information via an alternative interface.

Another approach that is taking hold is another industry buzzword; Service Oriented Architecture (SOA). It enables the development of an application from services which are clearly defined 'components' i.e. address lookup, customer add and credit check. So you can think of it as an approach that can link different processes together. An integration approach, very often using SOA, is a smart alternative to using a BPMS platform. For many organizations their problem is not about automating an isolated process or two, but actually is about getting the processes they have already automated working together in smarter ways. Our advice is don't assume that you have to have a BPMS in order to do BPM or to automate process. You may already have all you need but just have to get it working together better.

Choice

In any given situation, the person with the most choices will usually come out on top. It is our hope that by reflecting on what we have said and thinking about the questions in the next section of this book that you will increase your number of choices and thereby increase your chances of winning more often.

We have purposely only talked about the genres of technology and not about specific products. We believe that there are many great products out in the market today and that the only ones you need to know about are those that help you with your particular problem. We could name and slice vendors in many different ways, but ultimately the box, circle, quadrant or wave we might put them in is of little relevance. What is important is understanding what you need to achieve and then looking for the IT support – first internally and then to new software vendors.

Chapter

6

Ask the Smart Questions

If I have seen further it is by standing on the shoulders of giants

Isaac Newton (Scientist, 1643 – 1727)

SMART Questions is about giving you valuable insights or "the Smarts". Normally these are only gained through years of painful and costly experience. Whether you already have a general understanding of the subject and need to take it to the next level or are starting from scratch, you need to make sure you ask the Smart Questions. We aim to short circuit that learning process, by providing the expertise of the 'giants' that Isaac Newton referred to.

Not all the questions will necessarily be new or staggeringly insightful. The value you get from the information will clearly vary. It depends on your job role and previous experience. We call this the 3Rs.

The 3 Rs

Some of the questions will be in areas where you know all the answers so they will be **Reinforced** in your mind.

You may have forgotten certain areas so the book will **Remind** you.

And other questions may be things you've never considered and will be **Revealed** to you.

How do you use Smart Questions?

The structure of the questions is set out in Chapter 7, and the questions are in Chapters 8, 9 and 10. In the table you have the basic question, a more detailed explanation of the question and then the reason why you should care. We've also provided a helpful checkbox so that you can mark which questions are relevant to your particular situation.

A quick scan down the first column in the list of questions should give you a general feel of where you are for each question vs. the 3Rs.

At the highest level they are a sanity check or checklist of areas to consider. You can take them with you to meetings or use as the basis of your ITT. Just one question may save you a whole heap of cash or heartache.

In Chapter 11 we've tried to bring some of the questions to life with some real-life examples.

This is where you should find the real insights. There may be some 'aha' moments. Hopefully not too many sickening, 'head in the hands – what have we done' moments, where you've realized that you company is hopelessly exposed. If you're in that situation, then the questions will help you negotiate yourself back into control.

In this context, probably the most critical role of the questions is that they reveal risks that you hadn't considered. Risks that could seriously damage your business as we described in the opening Chapter. On the flip side they should open up your thinking to opportunities that you hadn't necessarily considered. Balancing the opportunities and the risks, and then agreeing what is realistically achievable is the key to formulating strategy.

The questions could be used in your internal operational meetings to inform or at least prompt the debate. Alternatively they could shape the discussion you have with the potential vendors of BPM solutions.

Once that strategy is set, the questions should enable you to develop costed operational plans, develop budgets or determine IT strategy.

How to dig deeper

Need more information? Not convinced by the examples, or want ones that are more relevant to you specific situation? The Smart Questions micro-site for the book has a list of other supporting material. As this subject is moving quickly many of the links are to websites or blogs.

And of course there is a community of people who've read the book and are all at different levels of maturity who have been brought together on the Smart Questions micro-site for the book.

And finally

Please remember that these questions are NOT intended to be a prescriptive list that must be followed slavishly from beginning to end. It is also inevitable that the list of questions is not exhaustive and we are confident that with the help of the community the list of Smart Questions will grow.

If you want to rephrase a question to improve its context or have identified a question we've missed, then let us know to add to the collective knowledge.

We also understand that not all of the questions will apply to all businesses. However we encourage you to read them all as there may be a nugget of truth that can be adapted to your circumstances.

Above all we do hope that it provides a guide or a pointer to the areas that may be valuable to you and helps with the "3 Rs".

Chapter

7

The People-Centric Process Management questions

Insanity: doing the same thing over and over again and expecting different results.

Albert Einstein (Scientist 1879-1955)

T RANSFORMATION requires a change in the way people do what they do. The need and benefits may be clear, but a catalyst and a project are required to deliver the changes.

Understanding the backdrop for that project is basis of the first Chapter of questions. How you deliver the project from a process perspective is the second Chapter. Even though we are talking about people-centric process management it does not mean that there is not a level of IT support, hence the final Chapter of questions.

Chapter 8: People questions

1. What's driving you
2. Organizational culture
3. The people in the process
4. Governance and benefits realization

Chapter 9: Process questions

- Project scope
- Resourcing
- Approach and standards
- Center of Excellence/Business Process Competency Center
- Process governance
- Communication, roll-out and continuous improvement

Chapter 10: Technology questions

1. Audience and devices
2. Enterprise architecture
3. Tools and applications strategy
4. Legacy process content
5. Delivery and deployment
6. Support
7. Vendor selection

Chapter

8

People

Failing to plan is planning to fail

Alan Lakein (author of How to Get Control of Your Time, 3m copies sold)

IT is madness to dive right into a process improvement project without really understanding the organizational and cultural context. For some organizations managing by process runs through their veins, driven from the top. In other organizations process is seen, rightly or wrongly, as the greatest inhibitor of innovation.

Where is your organization on that continuum? How will that affect how you run the project – or whether it is even worth starting!

What is driving the need for the project? Markets, regulation, competition? Or internal changes such as the implementation of a software application, outsourcing or M&A activity?

Most projects fail before they start. When they pick through the entrails of a failed project normally they find one of scope, timing or resourcing was never right from the start. You may have never run a process management project so here are the questions to ask before the project gathers momentum and becomes uncontrollable.

8.1 What's driving you?

What sets the context and business background for the
organization? Is it external regulation which sets the tone or is
market allowing the company to be a free spirit? Is the company
playing catch-up against larger competitors or is it the market
leader with smaller rivals looking to exploit any missed opportunity
or customer service blunder?

☒	Question	Why this matters
☐	8.1.1 Market impact	Do the market dynamics affect the organization or is the business relatively immune? Is change driven by customer demands or changes in customer demographics?
☐	8.1.2 Cyclical or seasonal markets	Does your business have marked seasonal changes which will determine the best timing for a process project which may require support from customer facing staff.
☐	8.1.3 Level of regulation	Are you heavily regulated by external bodies? Do your customers require certain levels of certification such as Quality, Security or Diversity? Is that level of regulation increasing?
☐	8.1.4 Market competitiveness	Are you in the fortunate position that you have limited competition, or is your world fiercely competitive? Are your competitors forcing you to change? Are markets or competitors consolidating? What is the basis of the competition – quality, price, speed, product, service, reliability?
☐	8.1.5 Level of customer touch	Do you deal directly with customers or are their intermediaries – VARs, distributors, retailers, websites, outsourced call centers?
☐	8.1.6 M&A	Is change being driven by M&A? Is part of the strategy growth by acquisition of products or companies? Is this changing – increasing?
☐	8.1.7 Outsourcing normal	Is outsourcing elements of back office normal? Alternatively are elements of your product/service development handled by partners? What about customer-facing activities?
☐	8.1.8 Markets geographically dispersed	Do you have truly global markets with product and price transparency? Or are you operating in multiple countries with specific market characteristics?

☒	Question	Why this matters
☐	8.1.9 Level of external change	Is change being imposed on you by external forces such as regulation, market consolidation price pressure?
☐	8.1.10 Internal level of change	Is change driven by internal drivers? A push to drive down costs or an acquisition or growth strategy?
	8.1.11 Whose problem	Where is the opportunity to drive improvements? Who owns the problem and do they understand how Process Management can help them?
	8.1.12 Why a problem	Is it understood why there is problem? Is due to rapid growth, M&A, a lack of attention to process, completion or customer demands?
	8.1.13 Current workaround	How are people getting around the current problems? Are they using documents, forms or spreadsheets using MS Office? Are they 'doing their own thing' locally? Is this a problem in terms of high cost, poor customer service or lack of compliance?
	8.1.14 Impact if not solved	If the problem goes unsolved what is the eventual impact? Will it continue to escalate beyond the current problem? Will the organization lose customer share or is it at risk of a compliance fine? Is it impacting staff satisfaction?
	8.1.15 Scale of impact	Is the impact localized or does it have an impact on the whole organization? For example a major compliance issue in a pharma company could result in a fine but also prevent the company trading.

8.2 Organizational culture

What is your culture? At a company we know well their culture is 'relaxed, yet professional'. That what their staff tell them. That's what their clients tell them. That's the exact wording in their company value statement.

In the office, from the CEO down we wear jeans, polo shirts and sneakers. Or whatever people want to wear. But when they go to the client they wear what the client wears – suit and tie at Nestlé, smart shirt and chinos at Microsoft.

But where are you? And as a newcomer to the company how do you make a judgment? And more importantly where is your company on the process-chaos continuum? Love process. Hate it with a passion. Or perhaps you tell people that you do 'get process', but then choose to ignore it at every opportunity?

☒	Question	Why this matters
☐	8.2.1 Process maturity	Do you deliver exceptional service through staff heroics, or is there clearly documented and understood processes and procedures so that live is calm and managed? How does this differ from department to department, country to country?
☐	8.2.2 Process reputation	Is process a "dirty word" Is it seen as an inhibitor to innovation? Or maybe there have been several high-profile process improvement project failures in the past.
☐	8.2.3 Level of resistance to change	How engrained are the current operating processes and entrenched are the staff? Just because there are a number of long-term serving staff it does not mean they are not open to change. They can see better than anyone else the potential for improvements. Or do they?
☐	8.2.4 Change driven from top	How does change get driven in the organization? Does it come as a top level mandate, and if so is it supported with actions rather than just words.
☐	8.2.5 Ground swell from grass roots	Does any initiative need to start at grass-roots and once it has proven value it then gets adopted at a more senior level? Does this vary by department, division or country?
☐	8.2.6 Change formalized as projects	Is there formalized process, including definition, business case and sign-off for any process improvement project? Alternatively, they may be informal skunk-works projects. Are managers given autonomy to run their own areas of operation? Or a combination of all of this – if so where does your project fit?
☐	8.2.7 Benefits of change measured	How are you going to measure the benefits of the project? Can you? Do you need to? How have other projects built their benefit cases and then have they needed to deliver on their promises?

☒	Question	Why this matters
☐	8.2.8 Leaders believe in process	Does the importance and adherence to process flow right to the top – or from the top down? Senior people tend to be numbers rather than process people. Big hands – small map.
☐	8.2.9 Leaders demonstrate belief	Even if the leaders do not look like they are following processes every day, do they still believe in the importance? The greatest demonstration is the allocation of budget and their time on the project – not just the project kick off with a ra-ra speech holding a glass of wine and an eye on the clock.
☐	8.2.10 Multiple change initiatives running	Are there always a number of change projects running? Is there an established programme or standard approach within the organization? Perhaps this is a new start-up, a dramatic shift in approach or M&A has changed the culture?
☐	8.2.11 Process driven by compliance	Is there backdrop of compliance and compliance projects? This may be good – known need – or bad – complacency or compliance fatigue.
☐	8.2.12 Implementing new software apps	Most organizations have an ongoing programme of software application refresh or upgrades. How does that affect the culture and acceptance of transformational change? How are these projects run – by IT, IT with active business involvement, by business?
☒	8.2.13 Strategy includes outsourcing	It is difficult to outsource something that you don't understand in process terms. Not that people haven't tried, but it normally ends badly and expensively. How has the organization's experience colored their judgment on outsourcing?
☐	8.2.14 Risk and governance	In some organizations risk, compliance and audit are being combined. Are they in yours, or is this being planned?

☒	Question	Why this matters
☐	8.2.15 Driving consistency	Is it expected that local operations are responsible for continuous change? Does this happen in practice or does it require a centrally organized and funded project to make change?
☐	8.2.16 Size of change	How great is the impact of the change planned? Is this big or small compared with other previous projects? Is it good or bad that the project has a high profile?
☐	8.2.17 Urgency of change	Not all change is urgent. It is a 'long march' where steady improvement is the key? Is there a burning platform driven by regulation, the markets or competition? How is the company reacting and is it consistent with the culture?

8.3 The people in the process

Is the end game automating a process so the audience for the process content is the IT team? Or are you trying to drive consistency of HR processes across all offices, so the audience is all 100,000 employees.

What are they going to access the process content on and where? On a 3Gphone offsite abroad is a very different proposition to the person in the field but in a hazardous environment, such as an oil refinery. Maybe they are in a call center. But is that call center virtual, so the operator is at home, in-house in a secure building or outsourced?

☒	Question	Why this matters
☐	8.3.1 End audience defined	Are you clear about who is the ultimate audience for the process content? Can you describe a 'day in their life' so you understand the use cases?
	8.3.2 Process project audience	Who are the participants in the process work? This includes the end user audience, but also the other stakeholders; process owners, levels of management, business analysts and IT.
☐	8.3.3 Multiple audiences	Are their multiple audiences with very different needs? Is every country the same or does legislation or custom and practice enforce changes. Are their different departments such as IT and sales accessing the processes? What about 3rd parties?
☐	8.3.4 What languages	What languages do you need to support, or is English the business language? That may be correct for professional in the organization but is that really true the frontline staff?
☐	8.3.5 Access to audience	Are you able to work directly with all the representatives of each user group, or are their intermediaries such as Business Analysts or consultants?
	8.3.6 Problem understood by audience	Do each of the audiences understand the problem that needs to be solved? Do they just understand it from their perspective or is their empathy with each other? What team-building is required?
	8.3.7 Audience engagement	How will you engage the different audiences and keep them hooked throughout the project? Many will be part time and will have conflicting pressures, and they still need to deliver in their day job.

☒	Question	Why this matters
☐	8.3.8 Process experiences	How much experience do the users have of working with the process content you are proposing? What is the learning curve and does this differ by country, division or department?
☐	8.3.9 Training for audience	What training on the principles of process management needs to be arrange, and in what languages?
	8.3.10 Resistant to change	What resistance is there to change in the different audiences? Does this need to be addressed in the training or team building activities?
☐	8.3.11 Process ownership understood	Is the concept of process ownership understood? Is it baked into the organization and reinforced through reviews and salaries/bonuses? How is process ownership across silos and countries handled?
	8.3.12 HR engaged	Has HR been engaged to support the changes to the organizational, designing rewards structure and job descriptions, and supporting union negotiations?
☐	8.3.13 3rd parties	Who else is supporting the project who needs to be considered? Consultants, contractors, software vendors, business analysts or partners?

8.4 Governance and benefits realization

Process content that is going to be running the business needs to be controlled. It will inevitably change, not just after the project has finished, but during the project. How are you going to control the changes and manage scope creep?

You agreed a set of benefits with the Board or Steering Committee to justify the project. How are you going to demonstrate the benefits over time? Ideally you will deliver a better Return on Investment.

☒	Question	Why this matters
☐	8.4.1 Project ownership	Who is in overall control of the project? Is it IT or lead by the head of a business unit? What political clout and experience of running project do they have? How much education and support will they require?
☐	8.4.2 Steering committee membership	Is there a formalized Steering Committee in place or do you need to establish one? What level of process knowledge do they have? Are they open to your ideas on approach or do they need education? What are the politics within the Steering Committee?
☐	8.4.3 Formal governance cycle	What is the governance cycle for getting agreement on project scope, scope changes, resourcing and status reporting?
☐	8.4.4 Managed governance cycle	Who is responsible for managing the governance cycle? If no-one steps forward it will fall to the Project Manager and the project team.
☐	8.4.5 Benefits realization costs	How will you demonstrate the benefits have been realized? Is there a standard calculation or a formalized approach; e.g. staff reductions plus legal, redundancy costs and an allowance for legal disputes?
☐	8.4.6 Benefits measurable	Are the benefits described in terms of reducing waste, cost savings (internal & 3rd party), greater staff effectiveness, improved customer service, better product quality or competitive advantage?
☐	8.4.7 Benefits already counted	Is another initiative already claiming these benefits e.g. software implementation? Do you need a business case or can you piggy back on the case of another project?
☐	8.4.8 Benefits realization	What mechanism do you have for realizing the benefits? Cost savings in facilities or equipment, services or 3rd parties can be shown. But do reductions in headcount mean really sacking staff or is redeploying good enough?

Chapter

9

Process

If you can't describe what you are doing as a process, you don't know what you're doing.

W. Edwards Deming (American statistician, 1900 - 1993)

YOU wouldn't start writing a book unless you were clear about who is going to read it and why? So why would you start a process project without asking the same questions? The answers determine so much that follows. The approach you take, the standards you adopt and how you ultimately deliver the process content, will determine the success of the project.

9.1 Project scope

Get this wrong and you will never deliver a successful project. Where to start? What is the ideal first pilot project? The biggest benefits are fixing a core process such as Quote to Cash, but if you are trying a new approach supported by a software application new to your organization do you really want this level of scrutiny. Besides, the sales teams are notorious for abdicating themselves from any processes.

So where can you get really adoption to prove the success of the project? Possibly a support process such as 'Inducting a new employee'? Sounds low key, but the benefits of a really slick recruitment and on-boarding process are greater than you would initially think. You get the best candidates, make job offers before the competition, get them on board and working effectively more quickly.

In terms of scope, if you haven't got it signed off by the Steering Committee you are at risk as the Project Manager. Scope creep, inadequate resourcing and unrealistic milestones are project killers.

☒	Question	Why this matters
☐	9.1.1 Project objectives	What is a 'great result'? For you, for the CEO, for the users, for the Steering Committee. Are they by any chance the same answer?
☐	9.1.2 Scope – geography	What geographies does the project cover, and what languages is the project expected to work in? Are the countries represented on the Steering Committee?
☐	9.1.3 Scope – business area	What business areas does the project cover and are they represented on the Steering Committee?
☐	9.1.4 Scope – internal & external	Does the scope cross boundaries – inter-division, partners, outsourcing partners or customers?
☐	9.1.5 Dead-lines and milestones	What are the critical milestones and deadlines? Who has set them and how set in stone are they? What happens if you miss a milestone?
☐	9.1.6 Project dependencies	What other projects are you dependent on? For example you require the new network to be able to use the multi-user process modeling database. Or do you need wait for a reorganization or new hire?
☐	9.1.7 Pilot, standalone or supporting	Is this a pilot project which is under the radar to prove the ROI and approach, or a high profile project? Or is it part of an existing project such as an ERP roll-out?
☐	9.1.8 Multiple change initiatives running	Part of a wider programme which has an established PSO and Steering Committee. Is that good or bad. Perhaps you would be better to establish your own structure?
☐	9.1.9 Greatest chance of success	Where will you get adoption most easily? This is the best place to start for a pilot project. Adoption is far better than the greatest potential ROI for demonstrating success.
☐	9.1.10 Compl-iance drives project	Is there a compliance driver for the project? If so – "Home Run". This is by far the easiest project to get funded.

☒	Question	Why this matters
☐	9.1.11 Implementing new software apps	If you are implementing new software applications then the first step is process discovery to drive out the package configuration needs. The challenge is it is likely to be an IT dominated project so they may look at the process content as purely the requirements definition and ignore its value beyond the project for business transformation. Also they may mandate a more technical type analysis tool and approach.
☐	9.1.12 Outsourcing part of strategy	It is difficult to outsource something that you don't understand in process terms. Not that people haven't tried, but it normally ends badly and expensively.
☐	9.1.13 Risk and governance is factor	Along the same lines as compliance this is getting a huge level of resourcing and recognition that process has a critical part to play. In some organizations risk, compliance and audit are being combined. Are they in yours?
☐	9.1.14 Waste reduction or customer service	Is this a more straightforward need to drive out waste or improve customer service? Does it get more complicated by crossing deeply engrained silos, divisions or countries? Or is it more ambitious and crossing country boundaries to outsourced partners, resellers or even customers?
☐	9.1.15 Need to drive consistency	How consistent are the operations across the business? Are different business units or locations duplicating effort with different tools for the same job /activity? Consistency of operation will make it easier to deploy the service.
☐	9.1.16 Potential for automation	Is this about simplifying a set of processes and then automating them to reduce the costs further and drive up compliance? Is the case for automation built or does the first phase of the project need to establish it?

☒	Question	Why this matters
☐	9.1.17 Size of change	How great is the impact of the change planned? Is this too high a profile for a new project or using a new approach or toolset? Do you understand the areas impacted and do you have buy-in or access to them?
☐	9.1.18 Urgency of change	The culture of the company may be one of slow change. But does this differ from the speed of change required for the project Is the project a 'long march' where steady improvement is the key? Or is there a burning platform driven by regulation, the markets or competition? How is the company reacting and is it consistent with the culture?
☐	9.1.19 Costs realistic	What costs do you need to include in your business case? Is there a set of guidelines? Do you need to add the time of part time staff 'borrowed' from HR, marketing, IT and Line of Business? Is it just time working directly on the project? What about attending workshops, reviewing content, attending training? If so what cost rate should be applied? What about their travel and expenses?
☐	9.1.20 Software costs?	It is easy to think that you can get away with using MS Office (Powerpoint, Visio) for process mapping. But using a tool designed for the job will save personnel costs in governance, collaboration and publishing. Have you added estimates for evaluating and selecting the tool?
☐	9.1.21 Senior level support	What level of support can you expect from senior management? Do you need to schedule training and education for them to increase their awareness and visible support for the approach you've chosen?

☒	Question	Why this matters
☐	9.1.22 Project risks – internal	Have you identified the internal risks? What are the barriers to success – culture, senior level support, IT tools, cost constraints, available skills, solid ROI.
☐	9.1.23 Project risk – external factors	Will changes to the market cancel the project? Is it 3rd party providers don't deliver? Maybe your major competitor's actions changes strategy or customer demands mean you can't resource the project.
☐	9.1.24 Risk mitigation	How are you going to mitigate the risk? Does that increase the costs, such as bringing in consultants to support the project team or providing senior management training?

9.2 Resourcing

How will you resource the project? Who has the skills? If you use external consultants how will you drive ownership of the project internally? And how will you develop the skills to maintain the processes after the consultants have left?

As you go through the Smart Questions you will realize that there are probably more people involved in the project that you first thought, if you want the project to be a success; project staff plus Line of Business, HR, IT and marketing

☒	Question	Why this matters
☐	9.2.1 Full time project team	Have you the mandate to form a dedicated project team? A part-time team will be a major risk. At a minimum there needs to be a core of 2-3 people full time.
☐	9.2.2 Project sponsors	Who is openly and visibly sponsoring the project? Are they at the correct level and do they have the political clout? Do they really understand the project and what you are trying to achieve?
☐	9.2.3 Comm-unications and marketing	Have you the skills in-house to drive a formalized marketing and communications plan? How much education do these people need and will they have the time or will they get pulled at short notice for client-facing work?
☐	9.2.4 Architect	This is probably the most critical role, especially if you have multiple process initiatives running concurrently. Their role is to coordinate across programme / projects and ensure that the different process content hangs together, has a consistent look and feel and uses project agreed terminology and standards
☐	9.2.5 IT integration	You will need to engage with the IT team at several levels. They will need to help you install and configure any BPM tools. There will be a need to integrate the process content with back-end systems and metrics to it can be access by the wider end user community. Finally, if you are intending to automate processes then this will require hands-on dedicated IT resources – no matter what the BPM vendor claims.
☐	9.2.6 Consult-ing support	What internal experience do you have with the approach, tools, business area, project management? Do you need to use external resources – full time or specialist consulting?

☒	Question	Why this matters
☐	9.2.7 Knowledge transfer	If you are using 3rd parties what plans are there to proactively transfer knowledge from them to your teams? Is this in the project plan and measurable?
☐	9.2.8 Internal customer - Line of Business or IT	What access do you have to your end user - the 'internal customer'? Are they senior enough? What education do they need on the approach and tools? Are they a cost to the project?
☐	9.2.9 Process owners	Does your company even recognize the term process ownership? Is there a formal process ownership structure? Are they committed to the project?
☐	9.2.10 Office space	Where is the office? A 100% virtual project sounds great but in practice people need to meet people. Certainly the central team need a space which is theirs.
☐	9.2.11 Remote working	For geographically dispersed teams remote working is the only way. Is the infrastructure required to make this happen seamlessly in place? Is it budgeted in to the project costs? Are the security concerns addressed? How is access for 3rd parties achieved?
☐	9.2.12 Multiple geographies / time zones	Projects covering multiple time zones cannot all be web-based meetings, although a huge amount can be achieved without getting on a 747. Is there sufficient budget for travel costs? What about internet and webex charges, especially from hotel rooms?

9.3 Approach & standards

Standard, formats, methodologies. With so many to choose from which is best? Is there even a best one? Not surprisingly it all starts with "What are you trying to achieve?"

Full BPMN or XPDL cannot be read easily by end users. Simple process diagrams do not convey enough information for an automation vendor to work from.

Therefore a combination of standards may be required, but what are the interchange standards? All great questions to ask of the competing software vendors. But you need to listen carefully to the answers as they will all sound the same – "Yes".

☒	Question	Why this matters
☐	9.3.1 Previous project experience	Have previous process projects had a positive or negative experience and what standards were used? Is the use of a particular standard part of the impressions left?
☐	9.3.2 Existing process content and formats	What legacy process content is there, and what standards did it follow? There are probably multiple databases / folders full of content all with conflicting standards.
☐	9.3.3 Overall principles	There are some approaches which are independent of modeling standards. These are top down hierarchical mapping and engagement by live workshops.
☐	9.3.4 Methodo logy	A project does not need to follow a formal methodology. But some of those that are popular in companies are LEAN, TQM and Six Sigma.
☐	9.3.5 Model standards	There are a number of modeling standards; BPMN V1.0 or 2.0, UML, BPEL, XPDL, swimlanes. Which standard you use should be driven by the end user audience and how you engage with them. What is important is not picking the right one, but making sure that everyone uses the same approach.
☐	9.3.6 Reusabili ty of models	Gone are the days of months of documenting Future State (To-Be) and Current State (As-Is) models, which are carefully documented and then locked in a cupboard at the end of the project. A more fluid, shorter cycle time approach is being used now. The rigor and standards are imposed behind the scenes by the modeling tools.
☐	9.3.7 Depend- encies on other projects	This is where the role of the architect is critical in defining modeling standards up front and the overall architecture. Then the role is to drive compliance.

X	Question	Why this matters
☐	9.3.8 Industry proven practice	Are there industry models that you can use as a starting point, or to reference? These may be public domain and freely available, paid for or provided by consultants – such as eTOM, AQPC.

9.4 Center of Excellence / Business Process Competency Center

The Center of Excellence (CoE), which is sometimes called the Business Process Competence Center (BPCC) provides a capability to support all the business process management initiatives. It ensures that there is a level of consistency in the approach and tools used and there is a higher chance of success. But can your project justify what seems to be an overhead? When the project finishes what on-going commitment is there, and how do you estimate the size of the team required? The key is to understand that CoE provides programme support to projects.

☒	Question	Why this matters
☐	9.4.1 Buy-in for a CoE	Is there a process maturity to understand the value of a CoE. Is the scope of the project broad enough, the complexity of the project, or its profile high enough to make it easy to understand the value of a CoE? If the object of a process initiative is to get people working to a set of common practices in a collaborative way across the org, can you afford not to have a common methodology?
☐	9.4.2 ROI agreed for a CoE	Have you budgeted for the resources, infrastructure for the CoE and have you built a business case for the value it will generate. The benefits include; co-ordination of team reducing rework, consistent look and feel improving end user adoption, centralized governance reducing training costs. Since the project ROI uptick achieved with a CoE approach may be incalculable, maybe you should assume a standard percentage of all project ROI is attributable to the CoE.
☐	9.4.3 CoE supporting multiple projects	Is the CoE supporting multiple projects, and if so has it already been established? If it has, does its scope, approach and standards match they requirements of your project? If they don't then why not?
☐	9.4.4 Can scale as projects build	Initially the CoE may be no more than a few hours from one person. But the effort invested in setting a framework makes it easy to scale up - to add more capabilities and resource as more projects come on stream. This should be factored into the ROI and budgeting. What is the cost of doing nothing?

☒	Question	Why this matters
☐	9.4.5 Scope of services agreed	What is the service that the CoE is delivering for the projects? Has that been agreed with the projects because if it hasn't there is a risk of duplicated work? Conversely what tasks and key deliverables does the CoE expect of the projects? Are they properly managed in the project plan?
☐	9.4.6 Reporting line	Who does the CoE report to? Is the project, the Project Steering Committee, the line of business sponsor or IT team? If you have a Business Architecture group, it would be a natural fit because the CoE is about programme management.
☐	9.4.7 Coach or mandate	What powers does the CoE have? Can it mandate standards, tools, approach? Does it have the final sign-off on the process content? Or is it coach /advisor / consultant to the projects? It's a leadership role, so it must have the power to mandate, to veto to coach and mentor. A process governance board with Line of Business is essential to provide the CoE Mgr with a mandate.
☐	9.4.8 Staffing at correct level	Do not underestimate the seniority required in the CoE. It is not a simply a project support office or admin function. It requires a team leader with strong business sense who commands the respect of the projects. Can you staff it internally or do you need 3rd party expertise? If so, what is the knowledge transfer process so you are not dependent on 3rd parties?

☒	Question	Why this matters
☐	9.4.9 Location and language	With projects and ultimately post go-live user in multiple time zones where do you locate the CoE? Do you have one per region and the related issues of coordination? What is the business language? Bear in mind that the scope of the CoE may mean that it can offer hands on-help which may not be possible through video-conferencing alone.
☐	9.4.10 Supporting infrastructure	Do the BPM tools support decentralized process development but centralized governance? Do you need to have access to video conferencing, and if so is it of sufficient quality? Are you able to use collaboration technologies to be able to support, educate and control the projects?
☐	9.4.11 Budget and capabilities	If you are supporting multiple project and needs to provide hands on consulting, training and support, is there sufficient budget? Are you being charged for video conferencing use?
☐	9.4.12 Charging	Who pays for the CoE? Is it a centrally funded resource, charging to the programme or cross charged to the projects? Do you have to justify the costs or produce monthly reports vs SLAs
☐	9.4.13 Post-project support	Once the project has gone-live what are the plans for the CoE? How is the business supported longer term?
☐	9.4.14 Estimating CoE size	How do you estimate the size of the CoE throughout the life of the project and then ongoing post-go live? CoE is programme management. It survives and is independent of projects and there can be a conflict of interest if project manager has authority over CoE.

9.5 Process governance

This is the "process of process improvement" and it needs to be formally managed and controlled. Shouldn't this be the first process map you create?

Whilst simple drawing tools such as MS Visio and Powerpoint have widespread use, their limitations such as lack of version control and publishing is well understood. Which is why there is a strong move to process modeling applications with databases / repositories.

☒	Question	Why this matters
☐	9.5.1 Defined governance cycle	Has the governance cycle been mapped, agreed and published so everyone is clear? Are the responsibilities of those who are in the review and sign-off cycle clear?
☐	9.5.2 Owner and control of governance cycle	Who is the process owner? Is it the CoE? If so is it the same governance cycle for all projects in the programme? Where does IT fit in the cycle?
☐	9.5.3 Intrusive governance	Is the process limiting and constraining? Does it drive longer sign-off cycles which stifles innovation? Does it prevent updates to process content being made because it is "just too hard" to get them signed off?
☐	9.5.4 Manage and monitor governance	Who monitors the effectiveness of the governance cycle and chases sign-offs and manages escalation? Is this a manual activity or is it supported by the collaboration and authorization functionality of the BPM application?
☐	9.5.5 Scope of governance	What are you controlling - process diagrams, attached documents, metrics, test use cases, training walk-throughs, compliance statements?
☐	9.5.6 Who performs governance	Is the review and sign-off activity delegated to process owners, end users, IT or is centralized in the project team? What is the demarcation of effort? Is this split driven by limitation of the modeling tools used?
☐	9.5.7 Manage multiple stakeholders	Can you engage all the stakeholders easily in the review authorization and sign-off process? Is through a simple webpage for sign-off or an iPhone/mobile app – bearing in mind some of the stakeholders are senior people, one the road with very little time.
☐	9.5.8 Sign-off sequence	What is the correct sequence for sign-off. Does the business or IT get the final veto?

☒	Question	Why this matters
☐	9.5.9 Escalate actions	When actions (sign-off, reviews) are not being done on a timely basis, and the project schedule is being affected, what is the agreed escalation path? What if the bottleneck is the project sponsors? Then where do you go?
☐	9.5.10 Hand-over post project	Once the project has gone live, if you want to drive continuous improvement you will need to run a governance cycle. Who controls it? Who manages it? Who monitors it?
☐	9.5.11 Training level	Managing the governance cycle requires a level of training. Especially as the role is to support those who are involved in sign-offs but do not need to understand the entire cycle intimately. Who needs to be trained and to what level and by whom?
☐	9.5.12 Outsourcing an option	Can the entire management of the governance cycle be outsourced to a 3rd party? Could they be completely offsite? What are the implications for on-going support vs. costs?

9.6 Communication and continuous improvement

The success of the project, any project, hinges on communication. Getting real engagement is critical with the project stakeholders; the project team, who may be spread around the globe, the other project participants who are part-time, and the end users who are the target audience.

Ask any marketer and they will tell you that it starts with a memorable brand that supports the brand values of the product. So what are the brand values of your project – or more importantly of output of the project after you have gone?

And once you have left is there the correct culture, reinforced by metrics and incentives and supported with the right level of skills to make continuous improvement a reality?

☒	Question	Why this matters
☐	9.6.1 Project success	What would be a success and can you describe it in a set of attributes or adjectives that the project team would understand, be able to repeat and live by?
☐	9.6.2 Brand of the project	Have you thought of a memorable brand, name and logo for the project? This will also live beyond the project as the process content will take on this name after go-live. If you can't think of anything you can go for *My{inset company name}* or *{inset company name}360*
☐	9.6.3 Comm-unications plan	Have you engaged your externally facing marketing team to design your marketing plan for the project or programme? Do you have a marketing professional on the team to manage and execute the plan.
☐	9.6.4 Sufficient budget	Have you budgeted for your marketing activities? Normally for internal projects this is overlooked so you may get push-back. Driving a change in behavior is tough but the benefits are huge, so don't be fobbed off with "You can have a page on the intranet, or one article in the company magazine or e-zine"
☐	9.6.5 Access to resources	Where are you going to get the marketing skills? If you get one of your marketing team onto the project what confidence have you that they won't be stolen back when the next marketing campaign or event crisis hits?
☐	9.6.6 Look & feel for all communications	Don't underestimate the power of a compelling color scheme, layout and navigation of the process content. It will transform the level of adoption with end users. And adoption is the biggest challenge. Again look inside your own organization for skills. How does the process content fit with your intranet and website design?

☒	Question	Why this matters
☐	9.6.7 Range of media	What different media are you able to use to publicize the process content; intranet, email alerts, paper, magazine, posters, town-hall meetings, gate-crashing divisional communication events, social media?
☐	9.6.8 Users find the content	Are their links from the intranet, Sharepoint microsites and internal blogs to make it easier to find the right content? How are you exposing process content (diagrams, documents, metrics, compliance statements) to internal search engines?
☐	9.6.9 Roll-out planning	Who is responsible for the roll-out? What dependencies are there – technology (BPM software, other software ie CRM, networks, hardware), other projects, organizational changes? Has it been budgeted correctly, but has the budget been eaten up by the earlier phases of the project?
☐	9.6.10 Scope of the roll-out	What is included in the projects responsibilities? Hardware and software upgrades and roll out, end user training, data migration, marketing and communications, CoE?
☐	9.6.11 No-go criteria	How do you know if you are ready to roll-out? Is there some user readiness assessment? What is the minimum process content to be able to have a big enough impact? Is the roll-out deliberately phased to keep it low key?
☒	9.6.12 Process ownership handover	How are you planning hand over ownership of the process content from the project to the end users? How will you schedule the training and support. How much 'parallel running' have you planned?

☒	Question	Why this matters
☐	9.6.13 Ongoing support and continuous improvement	How are you handling on-going support of the process content, the change and governance cycle and process improvement techniques? How are you going to engender a continuous improvement? How do you make this 'business as usual'? Is it written into staff employee guidelines or even their Employment Terms and Conditions?
☐	9.6.14 Metrics / incentives to drive behavior	What are the new metrics which are reinforcing the new working practices and are driving the process improvement culture?
☐	9.6.15 Go live training for end users	Who will develop and conduct end user training? In how many countries, in how many languages? What format is the training material, bearing mind that if the BPM application is upgraded then any screen shots may become obsolete.
☐	9.6.16 Training for 'admin'	The goal of process improvement means that someone, probably the Line of Business teams, will need to skills to redesign their processes. With more of the BPM toolsets claiming that the business are able to use them, then what is the plan for training and handover? What is the role for the CoE?
☐	9.6.17 On-going training	Training is often scheduled for the go-live, and little thought is given to training to new staff as they join the organization.
☐	9.6.18 External PR?	Is there a PR story showing how you are 'world class' organization? Could you benchmark yourself vs. competitors on Process Maturity?

Chapter 10

Technology

Business process management (BPM) can streamline customer interactions and realign overworked employees with a new aura of process efficiency.

Editor of "Gartner Predicts 2002: Application Integration and Middleware"

N O process management project can deliver lasting returns without IT support - even a people-centric process management project.

It all starts with the end audience, and from there you can determine what devices you need to deliver some form of process content to.

It could be an updated set of working processes and procedures in a laminated folder because the working conditions or budget / business case does not allow anything else.

Or it may be delivering a combination of role-based guided walkthroughs linked to documents, video and automated applications on a mobile phone. Or anything in between.

This will drive the technology decisions. Do you simply need process discovery tools? Or the ability to capture processes end to end deploy them to end users? Is governance a nice to have or mandatory? What level of automation is required, and do you have the applications in house?

10.1 Audience and devices

Understanding the audience and their needs will determine what devices you need to deliver some form of process content to. Can existing devices be used or do they need upgrading? What about the network or other parts of the infrastructure?

How does this differ by level of seniority, business unit or country operation? How will you deal with the wide range of devices that end users seem to bring to work and demand are connected to the network?

☒	Question	Why this matters
☐	10.1.1 Audience defined	Is it just internal staff or 3rd parties such as contractors, associates, partners or customers? Do you clearly understand the use cases? Maybe they don't know what they don't know. If that is the case, can you create some prototypes?
☐	10.1.2 Multiple audiences	Are there multiple audiences and have you a clear view about their usage patterns? Do they conflict? What commonality is there?
☐	10.1.3 Audience by business unit	How does the audience differ across business unit and level of seniority within a business unit?
☐	10.1.4 Audience by geography	How does the audience differ across geographical region and level of seniority within a geographical region?
☐	10.1.5 Range of devices	What devices are users intending to use to access process content: PC, Mac, netbook, tablets, iPod Touch, mobile phones? Whilst that may be the aspirations, what will actually happen? Do you have security or access policies which make some devices infeasible? Is issuing a dedicated device unacceptable?
☐	10.1.6 Different configurations by region, country, office or department	How consistent are the operations across the business? Are you planning to perpetuate differing approaches to common processes? Consistency of operation will make it easier to deploy the service. Is Cloud Computing the opportunity to drive consistency and hence operational efficiency across the organization?

☒	Question	Why this matters
☐	10.1.7 Support for o/s and browsers	Which operating systems and browsers are supported? What level of backward capability with browsers? For mobile this gets way more complicated with a range of screen sizes, operating systems and installation programs. Being clear about your position helps, but also separating the presentation layer out provides you with some flexibility for later unforeseen needs.
☐	10.1.8 Access be from multiple devices	How will data synchronization be handled? What are the implications of information on different devices being out of date prior to a sync?
☐	10.1.9 Offline access required	Some of your users may always be connected e.g. office workers. Others such as sales people may not and if they need access even when "off-line" then you will need to consider solutions that offer a hybrid approach with a central "hosted" service and a local synchronized copy.
☐	10.1.10 Online access critical to the business operation	When the connection to the service goes down, what is the implication? You must assume as with any IT service that the connection may go down. This could be for a variety of reasons; your network or outbound connections, your ISP, any part of the internet, vendor internet connection, vendor unplanned maintenance.
☐	10.1.11 Length of time acceptable for no online access	How will your business continue to operate and how long before it impacts your ability to work effectively? How long can you live with no access? Do you have an offline copy that you can continue to work with? When the service becomes available how do you sync if only one region has lost connectivity and others are still working live?

☒	Question	Why this matters
☐	10.1.12 Level of security or encryption required by device	Assume that every device type will be lost or stolen, either by accident or maliciously. What is the business and reputational risk if the data falls into the hands of the competition, organized crime or the press?
☐	10.1.13 Access by internal staff or 3rd parties	What are the profiles and security clearances of the users? If 3rd parties are accessing the process content is it on their own devices or a device you issue? If it is their own device how much control do you have over the configuration and the other applications running on it?
☐	10.1.14 Policies for offline security	Your existing security policies may need to be modified based on the information the service stores on the different devices. You need to be clear about the capabilities of the service and your operational approach and therefore your data strategy to be able to determine the security policies.
☐	10.1.15 English or multi-lingual	English may be your business language, but what other languages need to be supported? At head office you may believe that English is the core language, but down at an operational level in the regions is that true? And language can be one of the highest barriers to adoption.
☐	10.1.16 Apps or process content need localization	What needs to be localized? Just the applications or the process content. If the content is being accessed by very junior staff then it is probably not acceptable to expect them to work in English is English is not their 1st or 2nd language.

☒	Question	Why this matters
☐	10.1.17 SLAs for availability	There may not be a single answer, but it will impact your view on the SLA's for the applications. Do you need to allow for operations across multiple countries or time zones. Global operations may need a 24 hour, "follow the sun" service, businesses with a warehouse may have overnight operations, and even traditional 9-5 SME businesses may have home workers who will need access during the evening. A salesperson in Australia is not going to appreciate a service that is offline at 2-3am UK time every day.

10.2 Architecture, tools and application strategy

You have a grand plan for how the different tools, systems, applications will support the business. How do the new process management applications fit in or change the enterprise architecture?

What is your strategy going forward? Minimizing the vendors? Best of breed? Each country is autonomous?

As new tools and applications are being offered as a Cloud service, is this an approach which is part of the strategy? You may not have a choice, because business users can sign-up for the service without talking to the IT department – the Stealth Cloud.

☒	Question	Why this matters
☐	10.2.1 Stable enterprise architecture	What is the revision cycle for the enterprise architecture? If new applications were identified then what is the process for including them in the architecture?
☐	10.2.2 Gaps and needs	Are there known gaps in the products that have been deployed vs. the architecture? What is the process for adopting new technology and what is the expected timeframe? Is there a fast track approach?
☐	10.2.3 Use current tools	BPM seems to mean technology, and normally a new technology to be procured. The first question must be – what are the limitations of the current tools?
☐	10.2.4 Technology standards	What technical standards must be adhered to; ie Open Source is first choice, Java based applications, only Oracle databases?
☐	10.2.5 Corp standards	How do you break corporate standards if a product is the perfect fit? Is there a process so that you don't fall foul of corporate IT later on?
☐	10.2.6 Policy on Cloud Computing?	The questions on Cloud Computing are enough for a book in their own right. But the key point is that Cloud Computing changes many of the rules and make some of the architectural and policy decisions look antiquated.
☐	10.2.7 Front office / sales apps	What are you using for Sales, Marketing, Customer Support? Do you need to integrate with any of these products?
☐	10.2.8 Back office apps	What is used for ERP, CRM, Supply Chain, delivery, accounting, HR, IT, facilities management? Do you need to integrate with any of these products?
☐	10.2.9 DM apps	Rarely do companies have one Document Management (DM) solution. Documents are stored in DMs, on file store and on the intranet. Which of these do you need to integrate with?

☒	Question	Why this matters
☐	10.2.10 Portal and collaboration	Is there a core platform for you intranet? Is it based on a platform or hard coded in HTML? How will you integrate with it?
☐	10.2.11 BI, metrics and scorecards	What is being used for BI? Is it a formal BI toolset or is it MS Office? Which of these do you need to integrate with?
☐	10.2.12 Existing BPM tools	Do you already have investments in BPM tools? Are you clear about their scope, functionality and strengths and weaknesses? Are you using their full capability? Are you using their latest release? When was the last time their sales rep came in and talked about how you could get more value from your current deployment?
☐	10.2.13 BPM tools strategy	What is the strategy for BPM? Is it one toolset, or at least one vendor for all capabilities? Does one vendor cover all the bases? Alternatively is best of breed and manage the integration points?
☐	10.2.14 Mapping and discovery	What do you use for discovery, process modeling and process mapping? Are you clear on the requirements for these tools? If process improvement is a goal, governance and publishing are as important as the ease of use of modeling.
☐	10.2.15 Business Analysis	Business Analysis tools have historically been aimed at the BA/IT audience and therefore are often too complex for rapid discovery / mapping with end users. But their support for the modeling standards of BPMN, UML and BPEL are important for workflow / IT development.
☐	10.2.16 EA modeling	Who owns the Enterprise Architecture (EA) and how is it documented and maintained? Does this require a separate tool or are the modeling tools or Business Analysis tools sufficient?

☒	Question	Why this matters
☐	10.2.17 Simulation important	When and where will simulation and optimization be used? Is there a need for a best of breed vendor?
☐	10.2.18 Deployment to end users	How will you get process content to end users? In what format? What control over access rights? And onto what devices?
☐	10.2.19 Content Management	Enterprise Content Management (ECM) solutions deal with collaboration and document content and are often not set up to manage hierarchical process content. However the integration is critical as many of the applications are the default portal and are one of the key DMs.
☐	10.2.20 Learning Management	The adoption and understanding of company processes is a skills that need to be tested and verified, hence the need to integrate with Learning Management Systems (LMS).
☐	10.2.21 Risk and governance	Highlighting risk and control points is best achieved by mapping processes. But the management of the sign-off of risk control points requires a different capability.
☐	10.2.22 Cloud implications	Do you understand the implications of all or any of the above technologies being delivered as a Cloud solution? What does this do you enterprise architecture and tools strategy? Perhaps reading the *Thinking of… Buying a Cloud Solution? Ask the Smart Questions* book would be useful.

10.3 Legacy process content

Process has been around as long as companies have functioned. So it is likely that there is some form of process content exists in the organization. How accurate, well understood, liked, up to date and complete will vary.

Key questions are 'Is the content worth keeping?' If you throw it away how do you justify it, and who gets hacked off? If you keep it do you potentially have more effort persuading the owners to change it?

☒	Question	Why this matters
☐	10.3.1 Processes documented	Focusing on only the scope of the project, what is the process maturity of the areas you are looking at?
☐	10.3.2 Validity of processes	If there are processes documented how complete? How up to date? How well liked and used? How accurate? And how are you going to make this assessment? Hearsay, user logs, interviews?
☐	10.3.3 Process format	Has the process content followed any standards? How consistently have they been applied? Are they all held in the same tool or database? Is so is the same version of tool and therefore no compatibility issues?
☐	10.3.4 Owner of the content	Is there formal process ownership? Who "politically" owns it, or more importantly cares about it? Where is the project manager who created it – very senior, influential, protective? Can you use the process content or just ignore it? What would you really like to do?
☐	10.3.5 What value	How is value perceived? Is it the cost to create it, or the value people get from it, or how well it is used? A simple test : deny access for a hour or so and see who screams.
☐	10.3.6 How well used	How do you measure how well used it is? Are there user logs you can check, or is it all printed and on desk requiring site visits?
☐	10.3.7 Difficult to migrate	Unless you do a representative test you have no way of assessing the technical difficulty. No matter what the brochure says about the "Tool's intuitive import module" there is likely to be some manual tidying up. Getting an early view of that is critical.

☒	Question	Why this matters
☐	10.3.8 Estimate of migration risk	Run a simple test. When a vendor says they have an import facility, what does it look like when converted? How much effort tidying up, sort out inconsistencies between the diagrams and validating? What is the risk? How do you mitigate?
☐	10.3.9 Quicker to transpose	Whilst migrating process data may seem like the quickest route, how much time will be added transposing, updating and convincing the original owners to change it? Will you suffer from a lack of adoption or the negative baggage that came with the legacy date. Perhaps it is quicker to start again, building exactly the right answer, and gaining buy-in along the way.
☐	10.3.10 Offshore conversion	Perhaps offshoring or outsourcing the conversion activity may be a cheaper route (China, India, Eastern Europe). Either to run the conversion routines and tidy up or simply to rekeying.

10.4 Delivery, deployment and support

Business change really is only effective when people act differently, consistently and in line with strategy. So a critical part of BPM is ensuring that the changes to working practices, the new workflows and supporting applications are used correctly by staff, partners and customers. That means adoption.

Therefore thinking about how the information and underlying technology is delivered to them is critical. It should influence how the information is developed and how the applications are built.

"Oh no! Not another set of applications to support" is probably the reaction from a hard pressed IT department who are being asked to do more with less budget.

This may be another application in IT's portfolio but it may have different characteristics in terms of data types, data volumes, usage and criticality compared with other transactional applications.

☒	Question	Why this matters
☐	10.4.1 Phased roll-out or big-bang	What is the roll-out strategy? Is it phasing by geography, device, business area, user type? What are the roll-back plans if there is a problem?
☐	10.4.2 Wider roll-out plans	What is the wider potential? Could it be rolled out to all partners or customers through a self-service portal?
☐	10.4.3 Planning migration	What technical migration activity is there? What level of risk is there, and what are the roll-back plans?
☐	10.4.4 Costs of data clean up	Have you estimated the costs of cleaning all the data to be converted? Bad data carried over to the new service can create a poor impression on day one, impacting adoption. One thing is certain, without base data for the users, the acceptance of the service will be a challenge. Has the vendor experience of cleaning data in your format and volumes? Therefore can they estimate accurately or is a 3rd party going to need to be used?
☐	10.4.5 Internal costs of data migration	After cleaning the data, it will need to be migrated and tested. Do you need to include internal costs for this data migration? Your internal IT team will need to export the data and possibly support the migration. Building export/import routines, testing and running migration as just some of the activities.
☐	10.4.6 3rd party costs of data migration	Do you need to include 3rd party costs for this data migration? If your internal IT team are not available or capable of building export/import routines, testing & running migration systems do you need a 3rd party? Are you allowed to use them?

☒	Question	Why this matters
☐	10.4.7 3rd party resources need specialist skills	Some activities may require specialists with specific certifications or security clearance? Some of your customers may require you to use contractors who are approved to a specified security level (e.g. Governments). Or your insurance or warranties may be invalid if you do not use a "certified" engineer. These types of resources are typically in high demand and you will need to provide longer notice to secure their services.
☐	10.4.8 What DR / roll-back during data migration	Have you costed the IT infrastructure required to protect the data as it is migrated? The migration is the riskiest time. If the migration fails then what additional capabilities do you need to be able to catch it and roll-back to the previous set-up?
☐	10.4.9 Changes to content and apps	What is the mechanism for capturing process changes and enhancement ideas for the systems and underlying applications? Is there a central resource? Is it the CoE or through of the IT service desk?
☐	10.4.10 Demand for more	Based on the success of the project good word spreads. So how will you manage or prioritize the demand from other areas of the business?
☐	10.4.11 Network sizing	New types of data pushed around the network. So sizing vs. roll-out plans.
☐	10.4.12 Project dependencies	Do you require other projects or activities to be in place first? These may be change programs, organizational changes, new systems or upgrades, market changes, customer contracts or legislative changes.

☒	Question	Why this matters
☐	10.4.13 Upgrades to servers, networks and devices	What upgrades are require prior to roll-out? Are these scheduled or are there dependencies on other projects? Are these on the critical path for your project?
☐	10.4.14 Funding upgrades	Are the upgrades paid out of a central budget or charged to the business and under what terms? What if you decide to externalize the service to all your customers? Does that blow your ROI apart?
☐	10.4.15 Funding ongoing operation	You are now dependent on some software vendors? What are the software maintenance charges, and do you have to take the upgrades? Who pays?
☐	10.4.16 Costs factored into business case	Do you have to factor the hardware, network usage, software costs and maintenance into your business case? Have you?
☐	10.4.17 Conflicts with other IT projects	Are the upgrades to the infrastructure causing you to be in conflict with changes required by other projects? For example you need an upgrade to all browsers to enable a plug-in to work, but this upgrade will require an upgrade to the CRM solution and that cannot be scheduled for at least 6 months – if at all.
☐	10.4.18 Training for 'admin'	What training do the IT team need to be able to manage and support the BPM applications? What new skills do you need to hire in?
☒	10.4.19 Technical certification in apps	Is there a level of certification in the BPM applications that IT staff can reach? Is this career enhancing? Does it mean they are likely to be poached? Are their non-compete clauses in the vendor and consultant contracts?

☒	Question	Why this matters
☐	10.4.20 What SLAs	What SLAs is the business is expecting vs SLAs from vendor provides. Perhaps the vendor cannot cover all time zones so do you act as the central help desk? How will that work? What skills do you need?
☐	10.4.21 How do SLAs vary	If you have a suite of different BPM applications (mapping, simulation, execution) how do their SLAs differ. This may be ok as some are operational and mission critical. Others are project tools.
☐	10.4.22 Support desk requirements	What are you expected to offer the business users in terms of hours, languages? What can you expect from the vendors?
☐	10.4.23 Upgrades and new releases	Are you forced to take patches and new releases? How does that affect current operations including training materials which may include screenshots?
☐	10.4.24 Back-up, restore and DR requirements	What are the requirements and data volumes? These may be very different form the normal transactional or database systems you are used to supporting

10.5 Vendor selection

You have probably selected IT vendors many, many times before. So these questions will highlight areas which are different due to the nature of the BPM applications.

You are going to be potentially dependent on your vendor every hour of every day. So are they going to be around tomorrow, next year and for the foreseeable future? In a world which is changing rapidly, where even long established global investment banks disappear overnight, then we can have no long term certainty. But we need to make sure that we have asked the Smart Questions and assessed the risks.

If you are considering procuring a Cloud service, that is a very different proposition and you should also read *Thinking of... Buying a Cloud Solution? Ask the Smart Questions.*

☒	Question	Why this matters
☐	10.5.1 On-premise or Cloud	For each of the applications, are they offered as a Cloud service, only on-premise or both? Can you migrate between the two? i.e. start pilot as on the Cloud service and migrate on-premise for the full roll-out
☐	10.5.2 Project or long-term	Which of the applications are project tools and which are long-term operational
☐	10.5.3 Proven scalability	Can it cope with the data volumes and user volumes for the organization – ie every employee or potentially every customer?
☐	10.5.4 Industry models	Do they provide or have access to business process models for your industry?
☐	10.5.5 Support for methodologies	Do they support the approach or methodologies that you are considering using
☐	10.5.6 Process model import / export	Can the tools import the existing process content models and convert them into a usable format?
☐	10.5.7 Support for devices on roadmap	What is their strategy for supporting new devices such as mobile phones as new models appear?

Chapter

11

Funny you should say that

Laughter gives us distance. It allows us to step back from an event, deal with it and then move on.

Bob Newhart (Comedian, 1929 –)

B PM sounds great in theory. The last Chapters of questions were valuable – but not very exciting or engaging. They could hardly be described as fun. What the book is missing are some stories or anecdotes which bring the Smart Questions to life.

If we'd interspersed these stories with the questions it would have made the last Chapters too long. It would also have prevented you using the questions as checklists or aide-memoires. So we've grouped together our list of stories in this Chapter. Some of the stories are painful and expensive, which makes them even more valuable. I'm sure that you have your own stories – both positive and negative - so let us know them:

stories@Smart-Questions.com

Alcatel

Lighting up at scale:

A leader in fixed, mobile and converged broadband networking, IP technologies, applications and services, Alcatel-Lucent leverages the unrivalled technical and scientific expertise of Bell Labs, one of the largest innovation powerhouses in the communications industry. They work with service providers, enterprises and governments worldwide, providing solutions to deliver voice, data and video communication services to end-users.

Migration challenge

The challenge Alcatel-Lucent faced was how to provide a migration capability to support large scale network migrations for network providers. The change team was tasked with creating an entire Migration Organization from scratch, in only 6 months! The capability encompasses Solution Design which builds the capability based on the network migration requirements, Solution Integration which transitions the new capability into the operational environment and Operational Services which utilizes the capability to fulfill the migrations.

It is not often that a company selects a mission critical project with fixed timescales and heavy financial penalties as their first attempt at bringing together people, modeling tools and execution platforms on a new system.

The starting point for their project was of course people, but for them the initial "key" people were their customers, so in order to be sure they could address their needs they spent time with the customers and used their customer's processes as the starting point.

Against these they overlaid their own processes. This was a quick and effective way of identifying the gaps and any changes that might be required to accommodate the customers' needs.

Engaging end users

Aware of the risks of such maps and models becoming unwieldy or disconnected from reality, the team at Alcatel-Lucent took the time to ensure that the models they created were recognizable to the users. They saw this as a vital task, they also found it important to use the naming conventions that users knew and recognized (the change team was actually using ITIL as a basis but did not see any benefit in forcing people to switch to ITIL names for the sake of it)

The resultant system that they created is impressive, with each "Migration" they deal with comprising of up to 1,000 "mini-projects" running at any one time. Of course there was no way they could employ a thousand project managers, so they had to have a system that could do the managing for them, only involving people when exceptions occurred and to this end created a comprehensive dashboard system. This dashboard ensured that the management team was kept updated, but only needed to get involved when they were really needed.

Speed of delivery

The system that was created by the team at Alcatel-Lucent in such a short time appears truly amazing. Others who have heard about the detail describe it as a complete Business Change Management System. Their project included the analysis and design of process models, the subsequent implementation of workflows, as well as the implementation of a fully working management dashboard discussed above.

The main business impact on Alcatel-Lucent has been that the tools have allowed a very fast ramp-up of the team and migration capability due to full integration, user friendliness, ease and speed of customization. In comparison with other approaches or a manual implementation method, the solution has lead to substantial savings in the program are projected to continue to do so going forwards: low maintenance costs, increased levels of efficiency whilst the project portfolio increases.

Reuse across the world

In addition, the business impact of using the tools has been significant allowing for the structured processes to be used within Alcatel-Lucent's Migration Operations Centre's across the world. The tools require very little rework for different customer migrations and have limited the amount of delayed or failed customer migrations by ensuring the standard processes and procedures are followed. Given this, the levels of risk on all migrations have been reduced by 75% because the action areas to be monitored for migrations are more limited and manageable along with saving

Something that the team at Alcatel-Lucent don't talk about is themselves. In order to achieve such an undertaking required an extremely dedicated and motivated change team. That team also had to be well supported by management, the results shows that all of these things were present.

Lesson: If you put together a good team, provide them with the resources they need, they might be able to perform miracle for you too. They will however require you to be clear on exactly what it is you want or need. Also they will need you to both get out of their way and at the same time your support. BPM projects don't have to take forever and can provide a great return on investment in only a short period.

Arizona Public Service

Burning platform:

Arizona Public Service (APS) generates, sells and delivers electricity and energy related products and services. APS serves more than a million customers in 11 of Arizona's 15 counties and is the operator and co-owner of the Palo Verde Nuclear Generating Station (PVNGS) – a primary source of electricity for the Southwest.

Burning platform

A catastrophic fire at an APS substation that destroyed five transformers caused millions of dollars worth of damage, and required a rebuild of the substation. The fire impacted 400,000 customers, and resulted in a corrective action plan being approved by the Arizona Corporation Commission (ACC), which is an Arizona regulatory body. As part of the plan APS agreed to incorporate leading practices into its substation maintenance processes and to implement a scheduling tool. The goal was to increase reliability by ensuring the substations were maintained in an effective and efficient manner.

The Substation fire provided a burning platform, both in a literal and figurative sense, which required APS to look once again at Substation Maintenance and determine the gaps between leading practices and current practices.

APS also met a challenge because of company values. How does one incorporate change into a company with employees that have an average of 17 years of service? Or incorporating change into a company that is undergoing incredible growth. APS customer base has doubled every 20 years. In 1980, APS had 400,000 customers and, in 2005, customers topped 1,000,000. In 2020, it is projected that APS will serve 1.6 million customers. So, in the midst of this substation crisis, the company also had to handle more customers than ever before.

Leading practices

To meet the challenges of increasing reliability and becoming aligned with leading practices, APS identified leading practices and focused on documenting the current state processes and capturing issues, opportunities, gaps, problems and unanswered questions. Once the current state was captured, the group focused on addressing the issues and creating a future state process that reflected these leading practices. By capturing the information in a professional modeling tool the team found it easier understand the gaps and undertake impact analysis.

Beyond the technology a key part of APS's strategy was to identify and appoint Process Owners and they attended all of the process meetings along with process teams. Additionally the two layers of management above the section leaders also attended the sessions periodically to show support and provide the incentive from leadership. The "voice of the customer" was to reduce the number and age of the work orders and to implement a scheduling system that would support planning for five weeks out.

Leading from the front

Implementing leading practices required changes in how work was distributed and changed job duties. The leaders were exemplary in being there to support that what was being done was the "right" thing. They let people work through their problems with the changes but reassignment for people who were not in alignment was an option. Management provided a consistent message and culture change happened. Throughout all of this, the focus on process enabled people to envision what was needed to meet the ACC requirements and to become more proactive in their work.

In 2007 Substation Maintenance met or exceeded all of their reliability metrics. Before the process effort, they had not met more than 80% of the metrics. Before the process effort, 80% of their work was reactive, now 20% is. They have created acceptable ranges for the number and age of work orders.

Ongoing change

Following on from this project, the company has undertaken several more, all of which have been successful, and in 2008 Vice President for Energy Delivery started a major new initiative. The purpose of the multi-year initiative, which is process-based, is to assess processes, procedures, technologies, capabilities and organizational and operational effectiveness and performance to identify areas for improvement. The cross-functional areas included in the initiative include Asset Management, System Planning, System Operation, Design and Engineering Construction, Project Management and Standards, Design and Configuration Management.

Lesson: It is not until disaster strikes that many companies realize the value of having well documented maps and models of their business. And then of course it is too late. However, by having these things in place early makes it easier to assess the impact of change, driven by business needs or regulatory compliance. The company can also more readily adapt to change and ensure that everyone is utilizing the most up to date information and, as in this case, handle expansion more easily.

Gallagher Estates

People are the process:

Gallagher Convention Centre, one of
Africa's largest conference and exhibition venues started as an
estate for the Gallagher family. In its grounds of 30 hectares there
are 25 000 square meters of exhibition space, nineteen
multipurpose venues and state of the art facilities, Gallagher
Convention Centre can accommodate anywhere from 2 to 12 000
visitors.

The complexities are running such a large and complex people
centric business are huge, and because of the business domain they
are in, any mistakes are highly visible.

Made to feel like a star

So imagine for a moment that you arrive at the centre for the first
time, as your driver announces your name at the front gate you
notice a large sign with your name welcoming you and with
directions for you to follow. The security guard at the gate insists
on opening the door to see you and says he wants to be the first to
welcome you. Your car follows a route through the estate, all with
personalized signs, before directing you to a car park, where there
is a space with your name on it. As soon as the car is parked, you
notice that someone is stood waiting for you, your host? no
another security guard who welcomes you by name and invites you
to follow him to reception. As you arrive at a reception a smiling
lady gets up to greet you and shake your hand and asks you about
your journey. As soon as you are signed in the lady comes around
the desk and insists that she will take you to the meeting room and
on the way points out where all the facilities are, as well as chatting
to you as though you had known her all your life.

As you arrive at your meeting room, you discover that you are the first person to arrive. Well not quite as there waiting for you is an AV specialist who asks if he can help you set up your equipment.

Meanwhile the smiling receptionist returns with the coffee you were offered. So long before you ever meet the people you had gone to see, you have already been extremely well looked after. How would you feel about such an experience, would you feel good? Does it sound the sort of place that you might like to use again in the future? Are they the sort of people you would trust to organize your meetings?

Well the above experience is a true one and made all the more remarkable when you consider that the visitor was not a paying customer of theirs, but instead a supplier who was potentially selling to the organization.

People make processes work

It is easy when focusing on process management to think about maps, models and systems. When in reality it is the people who use those processes that will make the difference between success and failure.

For Gallagher Estates the emphasis was interesting, at a senior level they did not use process or procedure language particularly heavily. Instead they kept talking about hospitality and doing the right things. They also placed a very heavy emphasis on people communicating with each other. Certainly behind the scenes there were masses of policies, procedures and processes – you can imagine from a risk and regulation point of view it can get very complicated.

A by-product of this outside in, communicate first approach is that staff morale was very high. As they say themselves, you can't be happy dealing with visitors if you are not feeling happy on the inside. Of course if you do feel happy on the inside then it shows on the outside too.

The results speak for themselves

When questioned as to whether this light-touch, caring type approach was expensive and counter to running a good business, the company defense was robust and hard to argue with. In a highly competitive industry, revenue is up, repeat business is up and staff retention is high, meaning recruitment costs are kept low. While customer satisfaction and visitor ratings are at an all time high.

Perhaps, they have identified the real key to where to focus when undertaking process improvement.

Lesson: How do your processes look when seen through the eyes of your suppliers and customers? Are your processes communicated internally is such a way that everybody who needs to know does know? Focus less on the details of processes and more on the outcomes or results of the process. Good or bad, in the final analysis that is how others will judge you and your business.

Hindustan Motors

Next Practice in Action

Hindustan Motors Limited is part of the C.K Birla Group. The company was started in 1942 by Mr B.M Birla. In 1948 it began the manufacture of its most iconic vehicle – the Ambassador – the first car to be built in India (licensing the manufacture of the Morris Oxford from the UK). Over the years Hindustan Motors has equipped itself with state-of-the-art facilities for the production of passenger cars, trucks and multi utility vehicles. Today the company manufactures and sells cars for Mitsubishi and Isuzu, but still makes and sells the Ambassador, over 60 years on continuous production.

R. Santhanam, Managing Director of Hindustan Motors is totally sold on the benefits that process management brings to his company. He sees it as a crucial part of the company's strategy for success. However, Santhanam also believes that many of the advantages that process brings can only be gained by thinking about solutions differently. Hindustan Motors, also makes use of Next Practice and they were very keen to demonstrate the idea of Next Practice in Action.

Sumit Seth, the Country Head of Sales was eager to show off a new approach to car dealership and how they had applied next practice thinking.

High on Caffeine

Going through the car showroom and up some stairs one suddenly encounters enormous coffee shop! "High on Caffeine" complete with pool table, video games and countless other toys for boys to amuse themselves with. In fact the coffee shop was more like an entertainment zone with a café attached.

So why a coffee shop in a dealership and where did the idea come from? Well in the first instance they were thinking about ideas to increase showroom traffic. Then someone suggested that they were a little like a bookstore, somewhere people only went when they wanted what you sold. The rest of the time they stayed away. In thinking like a bookstore they realized that many bookstores had now installed coffee shops and turned themselves into destinations. Well, if it worked for a bookstore then maybe it would work for a car dealership.

At the time of writing the coffee shop has only been operating a short while. However, the coffee shop is already making a profit in its own right and they have already sold additional cars as a result of the increased foot traffic through the showroom.

There is more than just the coffee shop that makes this business model clever though; there is also the way they target who they want to visit the coffee shop. The company has very cleverly identified who would be potential buyers of the vehicles; the cars are at the higher end of the market and so the buyers need to be carefully targeted. They have then executed direct mail and magazine campaigns to attract just those who fall into the potential buyer niche and have ensured that the décor and entertainment in the coffee shop is designed to appeal to them.

Next Practice

For Hindustan Motors though, this is just the beginning, they are now looking at applying the same Next Practice thinking to the expansion of their dealer network out to potentially six hundred of India's smaller towns and cities, although starting with an initial twelve. In this respect they are now looking at having to deal with parts and servicing challenges far away from main dealerships and so are having to generate new ways of working and once again they are looking to other industries for their ideas.

They are thinking like a parcel company and looking at how the rail distribution and airport locations can help them identify which cities to target next. They also think of as not having mechanics to service cars but engineers, thus opening up the range of potential businesses who could act as local agents for the company. Other thinking is coming from areas such as Computer Maintenance – IBM have a great system of multi-levels of stores for spare parts around the world and the engineers travel with only a tool case, the parts being sourced locally for most incidents.

While other companies are still focusing on reductionist thinking, cost cutting and best practice, Hindustan Motors wants to be better than the best and is more interested in how to grow the top line revenue, this will reduce costs as a percentage of their business.

Lesson: Where do you look for inspiration and ideas? Is your company still inwardly focused only looking inside your own industry or do you look outside your sector and borrow ideas from other good companies? There are countless tales of companies who are seen as innovative or leading, yet when you look behind the scenes they are just copying and adapting. The only difference is that they don't just look inside their industry.

ING South West Europe

Compliance maturity:

ING South West Europe started a Compliance
Maturity program in January 2008, with the
objective of updating and improving the
organization's compliance function and where necessary improving
the approach and efficiency of Compliance Management by
process automation. It was apparent that several compliance
processes were very manual and resource intensive. As a
consequence new compliance regulations tended to result in
increased head count in the compliance area. One area of concern
was the huge increase in workload resulting from MiFID
regulations and ING urgently needed to address this in order to
avoid problems with the Belgian regulator "CBFA".

Motivation

A team of several regional Compliance Officers dealt with a wide
variety of compliance issues, including a (manually executed) trade
approval process known as 'Pre-Clearing'. With the implementation
of MiFID in November 2007, regulatory changes relating to
"Insider Trading" had resulted in an increase from 200 to 1,500
traders who must 'Pre-Clear' proposed trades. Existing ways of
working no longer sufficed. There were inconsistencies in how
different Compliance Officers worked. Manual intensive processes
and an over reliance on e-mail meant that the process was not just
inefficient, but impossible to report on from an audit perspective.
Monitoring was impossible due to the fact that all data was stored
locally in Compliance Officer mailboxes or folders.

A consistent and far more automated process was required which
needed to be followed by all Compliance Officers.

Cloud Solution

Capacity issues within IT meant that they would leverage hosted
process mapping software as a service capability so that no
software needed to be installed on ING's infrastructure.

However, the lack of IT capacity had another significant impact, which was that the IT department could not build the required process automation soon enough. If Nimbus was to be engaged by ING they had to not just define improved business processes, but had to automate them as well.

The first step was a process definition workshop with several of the Compliance Officers. From this ING and Nimbus captured the end-to-end process together with a clear understanding of the automation required. This gave Nimbus the confidence that the technical requirements were actually quite easy to deliver as a bespoke project. A technical specification was built from the process content, which after a couple of reviews with ING was handed to the development team who started work straight away in order to meet ING's deadline.

Result

The software development project was extremely fast, and 'right first time'. Compliance Officers access the 'My Page' to access the process descriptions, performance metrics and scorecards, providing a real time view of relevant process performance. A team of four Compliance Officers now operates the whole application as part of their regular job. Over 99% of trades requests are now dealt with automatically.

The process mapping software provided a process view which greatly facilitated the definition of requirements between compliance specialists and developers. Our cost per transaction reduced from €16 to less than €3, and we have exceeded our target for automatic processing.

Erik Werson. Program Director, ING.

Feedback from the Program Director verified that by starting out with a clearly defined business process, communication was greatly facilitated between the development team, management and users. Also it had been easier to determine the appropriate measures to focus on for the metrics and scorecards. The initial pilot was so popular, that additional users started signing-up before they were formerly invited to.

Future

A second process automation project, the "Insider Registration Process", has already been completed. The Pre-Clearing application is being rolled out across the whole SW Europe region. Several other banks in the regions are also now interested in the same application.

Lesson: A combination of process mapping to simplify the processes and then picking the right technology to automate has driven huge benefits. Which has lead to further projects. This is the power of picking the right project, the right technology and focusing on delivering results.

Intrepid Energy North Sea

Outsourcing par excellence

Revenues of £220m, profits of £60m, 24 staff (yes – 24).

Now I know the CFOs out there will have their calculators ready and be working out the profitability of their own organization if it were based on this business model.

It is a real company – an oil company operating predominately in the North Sea. Their expertise is in selecting and buying the 'plots of land' to explore, which are called sectors. Recently they bought sectors that contain the largest oil reserves in the North Sea – to date. They also are good at selling oil to the market. And they are very good at subcontracting and managing everything in between – exploration, drilling, delivery and distribution.

Industry expertise

They know the industry and are consummate outsourcers. Put another way, they understand their core skills, they understand exactly what it takes to do all the jobs that have been outsourced. They know them so well, that they are able to define the correct metrics (SLA) to manage and drive the subcontractors.

For example, for every barrel of oil you pump out of a field you need to pump in a barrel of water to stop the field collapsing and reducing its overall capacity. For every two barrels of water injected back into the field you get an additional barrel of oil out. Therefore it is critical that the water injection plant is operational 24/7.

Almost as important as the oil pumping plant. Unless water injection is an SLA, then the sub-contractor is unlikely to invest in keeping the water injection plant at this level of availability.

Coalface to Stakeholder Interface

The successful oil business I am describing put in place a Intelligent Operations Manual accessible by all staff long before we knew what it was called. They called it the 'Coalface to Stakeholder Interface'. This is their business mapped out in process terms, both internally and externally, with metrics and supporting documents linked in the correct context. It links the drivers of the stakeholders with the actions of the coalface. This is used by the internal team and the sub-contractors. It is manual not automated.

The Director of Engineering and Production commented, 'I was looking for a tool that would glue everything together so we could create a focus for the business and enable it to move forward quickly. We had a long list of capabilities and functionality we wanted. I'd tried to put it in place at a US oil company where I worked some 10 years earlier but the infrastructure and software costs were prohibitive'.

Postscript – Intrepid Energy North Sea was sold for $840 million.

Lesson: Unless you know your business intimately you cannot outsource with the level of precision demonstrated by the case study. With an understanding of process comes the definition of the key metrics which form the SLAs in the contract. That then drives the outsourcers with laser precision. And that enables a relatively small team to focus on their key strengths and drive staggering value.

Irish Life

Going digital:

Based in Dublin Irish Life is a large
traditional pensions and insurance service
company. They have 5000 staff in the Irish Life group and 300 in
the Corporate Business division. The Corporate Business division
is a supplier of employer sponsored pension schemes and has
pension arrangements with 3,900 employers in the country.
In the pension business you traditionally have long relationships
with your customers. In it is not unusual to have 30+ year
relationships with employers. The result is that this leads to a lot of
paperwork, all of which requires sorting, filing and storing. If left
unmanaged the results have a massive impact on the business, its
staff and its customers.

The Corporate Business division undertook digitization of the
division by using business process management techniques, shifting
a paper based organization into the digital world. This created
major changes in the way that Irish Life Corporate Business
operated.

In the initial stages the focus was on removing as much paperwork
as possible through digitization. This then provided the platform
for introducing automation etc. By moving all the paper into the
digital world it was easier to capture the routing of work and
automate much of it. The resultant lightened load for the
administration teams meant that the company was then able to
offer a better service, which is becoming a major differentiator in
our market.

The approach to this project was to go right across the business,
but to do it in a shallow manor, so that we were not trying to
change one process too deep. They focused on the capture, routing
and reporting elements of the work once we had completed the
removal of paper files.

The IT team at Irish Life is seen as part of the business, rather than sitting on the side lines. At around the same time as beginning BPM project Irish Life also began adopting Six Sigma for project management and made use of it alongside their BPM initiative.

Paul O'Neill, Head of IT & New Developments used constant engagement with the staff to ensure they all felt part of the process to ensure the project was a success. For Paul it was a case of communicate, communicate, communicate and to get champions in to each area. People don't like change; and Irish Life had to convince 300 people that this change was good. A lot of staff had been with the company for over 20 years. Many of them have been working in the same way for 10 or 12 years. So like everything involving change it required a measured approach with good and appropriate communication.

The real magic of BPM is it has allowed Irish Life to integrate existing systems to get the real information we have out of their systems. The company has now added business intelligence (BI) tools and are using these to analyze how long processes take. This means they can put a real ROI on the use of BPM. They suggest that the information they have on their business and its processes they could not have had before.

Whilst the project was underway the business was growing so even as a result of improved efficiency, they didn't have to lose any people because they were able to be redeployed due to the growth of the organization. Paul also notes that they have seen an increase of productivity of 35 per cent.

Perhaps one of the best ways to gauge the success of the project is from an employee perspective. The number of workers who've come back to work from maternity leave, for example, and say it's a much better place to work is astonishing.

Irish Life is now at a stage where everyone is very engaged with this, they have a suggestion box with six to nine months worth of process changes in it. The result of this is a constant stream of change going on because there has been a mindset change, people talk about processes rather than work or tasks.

Lesson: By involving people in the process then the barriers to change can simply melt away. People, when working well together as part of the process, will usually deliver far more than you ever thought possible. In this case Irish Life achieved was is termed as the BPM triple crown, reducing costs, improving customer service and increasing revenue.

JPMorgan Investment Bank Technology Service Delivery Solution

Process & Systems Optimization in IT:

This case study outlines how JPMorgan, one of the world's leading investment banks, used process mapping and deployment technology to help improve service delivery efficiency within its Technology Group.

Global economic conditions have forced all financial institutions to focus on efficiency. JPMorgan's Head of IT identified that IT Service costs were high, when comparing the ratio of cost per fulltime employee served. A baseline productivity review was carried out, which identified a lack of standard processes across international offices, poor visibility of service performance (metrics), and a plethora of different IT tools used to deliver the services involved. Many had similar or overlapping capability, and it was apparent that significant on-going savings might be made if an appropriate way could be found to consolidate the tools used, whilst moving towards more consistent, best practice business processes.

ITIL based process work

A process and tools work stream was created to understand the current state; develop and as far as possible standardized support processes, and define a future state architecture. ITIL was chosen as a best-practice reference point with which to consider the optimization efforts. The work stream not only addressed the strategic service delivery processes, but also examined the inventory of IT tools with the goal of consolidation and standardization.

A process mapping tool was selected to support which was already used within JPMorgan where its suitability had been proven for a geographically-dispersed project team. Its simple mapping standards made process information easily accessible to everyone without the need to learn another 'technical' application. Its analytical capabilities were ideal for the identification of tools used against each business process, and the subsequent reporting needed to validate proposed rationalization scenarios.

The built in change control and web publishing would also ensure that the effort expended by the team creating, agreeing and approving new processes would result in a sustainable "process operations manual" for continued use and long term business benefit.

Solution

Initially, it was used to define standard ITIL workflows and compare the various (and often necessary) process variations. Whereever possible future state operating practices were consolidated around a standard best practice approach. The team then used it to socialize the proposed future state with the widely dispersed project members and stakeholders, to gain consensus. Having identified, communicated and to an extent agreed upon the new proposed business processes, the content was used to support the review of IT tool capability against the process context.

The process content provided a very visual indication of how well certain tools supported required "activity steps", which could be color coded (red, amber or green) accordingly. The goal was to eliminate tool overlap and duplication, whilst ensuring the new business processes would still be supported as required.

Results

The process mapping application was a key project enabler, providing a process analysis and communication platform which supported the Technology Group as they consolidated 48 Service Delivery tools into 4. This has also enabled improved performance reporting, which now drives productivity and efficiency programs across the division. The process content is actively used and maintained on an on-going basis, for service optimization and innovation.

Having a governed and robust approach to business processes management, together with a clear understanding of the tools used to deliver required automation will help the Technology Group maintain efficient operations and prevent the return to unnecessary disparate ways of working across the regions.

Future

The process system has provided a governance framework for the ongoing maintenance of Service Delivery processes, so that they can more easily be kept up to date. The resulting process operations manual is a trusted 'source of the truth' regarding how the division operates; which is already being leveraged and extended in ancillary projects. The specification of related system enhancements and additions is now more easily and accurately achieved in the context of end-to-end business processes. Such projects and enhancements should lead to further productivity and efficiency improvements for the bank.

The mapping application, with its ease-of-use and comprehensive functionality, has been and remains a major contributor in our mission to standardize processes and successfully drive change throughout the organization.

Rob Locurto, VP - Global FX Service Delivery Manager

Lesson: IT-led projects can learn from existing business-driven process improvement projects. They can use the tools and approaches rather than using their systems development modeling tools or jumping straight into automation. In fact, this project has driven out the benefits without developing new automated systems.

Newcastle Building Society

Meeting everyone's needs:

Newcastle Building Society is one of the U.K.'s leading mutual building societies with assets of more than £4.5 billion under management. The society provides a range of products and services including mortgages, savings and investments, financial planning and insurance. With a reputation for embracing innovative technology and developing groundbreaking products, the Newcastle has more than 1,000 staff and is the largest building society in the North East of England.

Expansion and growth can be challenging at the best of times, but with limited management information, and managers spending hours assessing queues and prioritizing and allocating tasks, it can be seen as almost impossible. This was the scene at NBS. In addition just like many other organizations their departments worked in silos and it this made it difficult to share resources when workload was heavy.

Customer focused

Their initial objectives were to improve customer service and move toward a more customer centric business. Secondly they wanted to break down silos and help to balance workload. So the initial idea was to replace manual, paper-based systems with an integrated automated solution. People played a major part in the success of NBS, as they moved forward into the realm of process; they stayed very focused on ensuring that the solutions worked at many levels.

For example, as part of the solution NBS developed their own management information system. It operates in real time 24/7 allowing managers to produce reports by department, team, individual, work type or process in just seconds. Mangers love the fact they now know exactly where they are. They are also able to see how much work is costing and measure overall efficiency much better. Because all work is now visible, they can continually improve efficiency by reducing the time to complete a task. This ensured that very quickly managers were on side with new ways of working and new systems, they could see what was in it for them.

Multi-skilled workforce

Training played a major part in the NBS process success story. Taking the time to multi-skill the workforce has provided them with far greater flexibility. With a fully flexible workforce – people can build up their skills in different areas and there are now multi-skilled teams working together. From an individual's perspective they are no longer expected to handle peaks in workload on their own, now there are up to 500 others who can help if needed. This has enhanced job satisfaction and boosted morale, as a side issue this focus on benefits to the individual decreased the resistance to change. In addition, for those who want it, home-working has become a possibility with staff able to access work from home, as you can imagine giving staff greater choice always goes down well.

Many of the benefits gained at NBS went beyond those traditionally associated with technology; they found that by moving to a more process managed organization they gained in ways they might not have anticipated. Process management was pivotal in enabling the executive team to convince the Board of Directors that they had the people, tools and capabilities that would allow them to diversify into new markets. Without process management in place, they could not have achieved that.

In addition to being better able to manage multiple brands, multiple product launches, new promotions and the peaks and troughs of market demand. The company now has the capability to get a new product to market within 16-20 days and flex resources to meet their SLAs. In addition NBS are now offer back office, processing and call centre services to other financial institutions. The ability to offer both member and third party services is a big differentiator in the market.

A process culture

NBS now feels that process management has now become part of their infrastructure and embedded into the culture of their organization, they believe it has become fundamental to how they organize their teams and how they operate.

Efficiency gains and cost reductions are very important to NBS but adopting a process management approach and opening up new opportunities and new business streams is what has really excited and motivated people. They see that the best way for them to protect their business and their jobs is through growth.

Lesson: By taking time to involve people at every level and ensure that the solutions you propose meet their needs you increase your chances of success. When dealing with the needs at the CxO level you may very often find that business growth is of more interest that cost saving. Of course if you can offer them both so much the better. Also we see that the changes for staff that lead to a better quality of life are more interesting to them than just a new way of working.

Sayga Flour

When Management Take The Lead:

Sayga Flour is part of the largest private company in Sudan. Their biggest competitor in the flour business is the Sudanese government. Some years ago they decided that in order to remain competitive they needed to move to a more process centric way of working.

Most observers of BPM agree that to really make the deep changes required for an organization to see the full benefits BPM can bring the top management team need to take the lead. This is something that Sayga CEO, Ihab Latif, understood well. He also understood that in order to make changes he had to invest in his people, to show them that not only was he serious but that he was willing to back the idea with investment.

Kick off event for 30 managers

After providing training some of his key people, the business and process analysts, he was ready to introduce the concepts to the managers in the business. To this end a presentation and workshop format was agreed and an outside speaker was invited and the audience size agreed a presentation for 30 people and a workshop for 15 people. In order to kick-start things Latif agreed to send out the initial email invite to attendees. The following paraphrases that email;

"As you are aware I am sponsoring the presentation *Why BPM and Why BPM for Us?* The reason I am doing this is my belief that the difference between good and great companies is the systems which are driving them. I believe that the presentation and workshop that follow will give all of us an insight into the management techniques used to analyze and optimize our business processes. As managers this should be a fundamental part of what we do every day.

The reality though is that we get bogged down in day to day details and do not detach ourselves enough to look at the reasons why we do things the way we do them and consider doing them differently. We do not manage business processes. We let the processes manage us.

I am hoping that this presentation will be an eye opener in this area. I am also hoping to increase awareness as well as give you a view on how as a company we want to take our management to a higher level by instilling BPM as a core activity and competence within the business.

I appreciate your commitment to attend and your further commitment to go through the change process which BPM can deliver."

The email was duly sent out. The result was astounding, not just the top team of the Sayga decided to come along, but so did the top team of their parent company and many of their other subsidiaries.

Turnout of 150

Instead of a presentation for 30 people they had 150 of DAL Group's top management assembled for the day. The event was a momentous occasion, the first time that such a gathering had occurred at the company, and the topic that they were so keen to learn about was BPM and process improvement. What a signal it sent out to the rest of the organization. Management was not leading with words, but was leading by example.

There can be no mistaking the vision and foresight of a CEO like Ihab Latif. Few other organizations with a 70% market share, growing revenues and profits would undertake BPM. In Ihab's words "It is no good waiting until we are on the way down, it is while we are on the top of our game that we need to make the changes. For at that point we still have the time and resources to make sensible, rational choices, rather than having to rush into things in the vain hope that it can save us after the fact."

A few days later when the first two day process workshop was scheduled they had to turn people away at the door. So enthusiastic were people that over 40 tried to attend and were actually upset when the last 10 had to be physically turned away.

Lesson: As a manager or executive, where you spend your time will signal to others what your real priorities are. If you are involved in process improvement they will get involved in process improvement. All too often managers only get involved by way of memos, emails and presentations. Each of these can help, but there is no substitute for actually getting involved.

Screen Actors Guild

Simplify and automate:

The SAG-PPHP was established in 1960, as
the result of a collective bargaining
agreement between producers in the motion picture and television
industry and the Screen Actors Guild. The SAG – PPHP benefit
participants and their families throughout their careers and into
retirement. Health Plan benefits include
hospitalization, major medical, dental, mental health, and chemical
dependency benefits and life insurance. The plan also provides
pension benefits to qualified participants. Benefits are provided to
working and retired actors and their dependents in all 50 states.

The Screen Actors Guild – Producers Pension and Health Plan
(SAG-PPHP) processes more than 750,000 medical claims with the
number growing each year. Additionally, it must manage a constant
influx of new member documentation.

A BPM solution

The BPM solution enables SAG-PPHP to convert paper
documents into easily manageable electronic documents, enhance
processes, and reach HIPAA compliance. They have
reduced the number of steps in the process from 26 to 6.
Additionally, SAG-PPHP has integrated its OCR software, claims
system HIPAA exchange server, and the BPMS into a seamless
process management system. This allows SAG-PPHP to balance
workload, integrate audit points into the process, and quickly
retrieve claims documentation.

With 66,000 eligible participants and dependents, the SAG-PPHP
must handle a huge volume of documentation: earnings reports
from the studios, performer information forms, beneficiary forms,
supporting documentation, correspondence, and claims. In
particular, SAG-PPHP processes more than 750,000 medical claims
each year — a number that continues to grow — while also
managing a constant influx of new member documentation.

Driving up workload efficiency

Processing such a volume of claims could be an overwhelming task for this in-house organization. But with a BPM solution the SAG - PPHP team handles the workload efficiently and cost effectively— while ensuring compliance with the Health Insurance Portability and Accountability Act (HIPAA).

Our focus this past year has been ensuring HIPAA compliance. A central part of HIPAA compliance is being able to receive 837 transactions electronically.

Amanda Bernard, Executive Project Manager for the SAG Producers Pension and Health Plans

They integrated the OCR software, claims system, HIPAA exchange server, and the BPM system. The BPM vendor's professional services organization set up and customized adjudication so the system will audit the automated claims process and facilitate error correction.

For example, should a problem be detected with a claim, manual intervention is required. Again working with professional services, SAG-PPHP were be able to transform 837 electronic data from the claims system into formatted images that can be viewed alongside other supporting documentation on an adjuster's screen.

This capability enables the adjuster to determine the problem, correct the information using a form within the process, and send the corrected claim back into the mass adjudication system.

Our top priority is to serve the needs of our participants. The BPM solution enables us to process our claims more accurately, more efficiently, and to provide the level of service our participants expect.

Amanda Bernard, Executive Project Manager for the SAG Producers Pension and Health Plans

Lesson: By focusing on process simplification first, you can speed up the time taken to reduce the cost of automation. Further, the benefits of a smaller, lighter automation also result in reduced on-going maintenance of the system. The historical approach of *automate first* builds fat into the system and can make it difficult to change, especially if the people who were in the process are no longer available to you.

Toyota Motor Europe

Lean Operations:

Toyota Motor Europe (TME) launched the Lean Operations Project with the aim of improving the European Sales Group "ways of working" to ensure profitable growth. The vision was to identify and implement structural efficiency and create a cost conscious mindset throughout the organization. The project is on-going.

"Lean Thinking" has a key role to play in order to adapt to the 2008-09 economic crisis which has particularly hit the automotive sector worldwide. It was essential to rethink current organizational structures and behaviors. The goal - strong performance despite the rapidly changing business environment and challenging market conditions.

Achieving efficiency improvement through "kaizen" (continuous improvement) and elimination of "muda" (waste) is a key part of the "Toyota Way" and in this challenging environment it remains a key priority within TME.

The approach for identifying projects needed to become even more pragmatic and aligned to "hoshin" (annual objectives), staff daily jobs and individual team objectives.

Solution

Toyota applies flexible criteria for improvement project selection, based on three key parameters:

- Alignment with today's strategic priorities. Any new project must bring immediate benefits.
- Measurement of Efficiency. Clear KPIs must be determined to ensure efficient PDCA cycle.

- Cross-functional projects. Multi-disciplinary improvements requiring high level coordination

Cross-Functional projects remain the key priority, however using a process mapping application enables numerous functional teams to drive efficiency & profit initiatives in a self-reliant and consistent manner. Toyota have branded it internally as "iMap" which is both the toolset and methodology now recommended for the improvement and communication of business processes. This provides a "Kaizen Platform" to support lean thinking, competitiveness and agility – critical in the current economic climate.

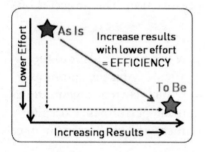 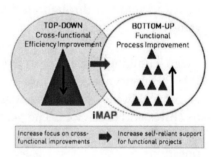

The capability has been applied to over twenty projects over the last five years with solid results. Some examples include:

- Product Lifecycle Management – maintain / increase sales before new vehicle launch. Increased process transparency for product Improvement.

- Weekly Sales Reporting - significant timesaving to provide weekly consolidated report for 27 country network. (ROI Euro six figures.)

- Marketing Images & Materials – Significant process acceleration for production, consent, approval and improvement of marketing materials across Europe. (ROI undisclosed.)

iMap delivers a flexible platform in which to visualize and improve processes on a Pan European, cross functional level but also at an individual staff level through iMap without large investment in special teams. Built on a customer 1st mindset it is a tool that allows us to meet quickly changing customer expectations.

Toyota Motor Europe

Lessons: The approach you use needs to be specific to your company culture, history, organizational structure and objectives. You cannot look at one company and copy their approach and hope it will work. Once you have chosen your approach and toolset you then need to embed it in your organization so that it becomes a way of life.

Chapter

12

Final Word

You can analyze the past, but you need to design the future. That is the difference between suffering the future and enjoying it.

Edward de Bono (Author, 1933 -   )

THE Industrial Age is said to have lasted around 100 years. The initial 30 or 40 years of that period produced inventions that transformed the way people worked. At a personal level those changes had a massive impact on the people involved in such work and the way they lived their lives.

Depending on one's perspective, people were slaves to the business owners, generally living and working in poor conditions. It was only during the middle of the Industrial Age that we started to value people and question the way in which they were treated.

Then as the age ended we were able to use the earlier inventions in ways that literally transformed lives for the better. Better housing, better health, better education and a cleaner environment.

Now we are in the Technology Age, we may have forgotten some of those values and gone backward by aiming to simply automate people. In the Industrial Age we tried to turn people into machines. This time we are thinking of them as extensions of computers. Just as things changed at the end of the Industrial Age, we are now at a point within the Technology Age where once again we need to get back to valuing people.

Our hope is that as you go forward in your business, you will try harder to ensure that the systems we build or the processes we implement will help people to achieve their dreams, to realize their goals and fulfill their ambitions. We are at a turning point where the technology that we create needs to focus more on enabling us to do things we hadn't even thought of, rather than simply automating what we already do. It is the former that will lead our businesses forward with renewed prosperity; the latter will see us continuing to spiral downwards to the point of non-existence.

We like you are just people too. We share similar hopes, fears and emotions. All any of us want at a very personal level, is to be able to feed and care for our families and friends and to live happy, healthy lives. So as you go on your own process journey, all we ask is that you think about the impact of the changes you make on lives others and how through your own work you can enrich your own life and the lives of the people around you.

Appendix: Running senior level workshops for process

A key part of any people centric process management project is the ability to drive out a clear view of end to end processes in live workshops, often with senior people. In our experience this can be tough, and the more senior the audience the worse it gets. So here are some thoughts on running those workshops

Preparation

- Company mission/vision/strategy from Chairman's Report in Annual report or website
- Scope of project from project proposal and scope document
- Objective of workshop from project sponsor or project manager (PM)
- Personal objectives of CEO, project sponsor and project manager (PM)
- Scope & context of workshop
- Audience – name, role, title
- What personal conflicts & politics in the group, and where is power
- Terminology – what will turn them on, turn them off, no-no's
- How much understanding & buy-in does the audience have of processes
- What is the pain to resolve
- Where is ROI or win

Agenda/sequence

- Introductions – go around the room
- Introduce session – why they are there, pain …
- Objectives of the session – working meeting to get a result
- Benefits of session –

    o defines company operational strategy

    o sets context for specific projects

    o sets priorities for improvement projects

    o kick start projects

    o identifies project sponsors and support

- Show 'finished product' - so they know what they are aiming at
- Strategic objectives on white board (tangible – with measures)
- Mapping from end point back
- Identify process owners
- Identify priority processes for initial projects
- Next steps

Conducting Mapping

- Important thing is get interaction and momentum – get them talking/arguing
- Start with blank sheet
- Start at back end of process "bill and collect payment" because it is easy, non-contentious and it gets the ball rolling
- Then move forward "what allows you to create the invoice"
- Don't worry about inputs and outputs initially, but as the debate grows between audience about the context and scope of each activity use the input and output to define.
- Use notes to document what the lower level activities are (if and when they get talked about) – try to avoid drilling down as it distracts from the top level
- To get them to focus on activities use "I have just joined your organization as a XXXX, and I need to XXX. How do I know what to do next? How do I know when I've finished"
- If they can't agree, move to a whiteboard to sketch a flow of processes, then go back and map

Issues, objections

- Can't agree on certain activities
    - o   revert to white board
    - o   try to define inputs & outputs
    - o   look to CEO/sponsor to resolve
- Don't have the correct people in the room
    - o   check if workshop results will be 'agreed'
    - o   look to CEO/sponsor to resolve
- People focus on departments or reporting lines not processes
    - o   Ask the 'I do XXXX, how can I understand what to do?' questions
- IT-focused people describe in systems (automated process) terms rather than the complete process
    - o   Ask the 'I do XXXX, how can I understand what to do?' questions

Other books by the authors

Mark McGregor's books

In Search of BPM Excellence,
MK Press, ISBN 0-929652-40-1

Thrive! How to Succeed in The Age of The Customer,
MK Press, ISBN 0-929652-41-2

Winning With Enterprise Process Management,
Aardvark, ISBN 1-4276-1224-2

Extreme Competition
MK Press, ISBN 0-929652-38-2

Additionally has developed and delivered a number of critically acclaimed seminars and workshops including;

- The People Side of Change
- People Centric Process Management
- Mapping & Modeling for the 21st Century

Ian Gotts' books

Common Approach, Uncommon Results,

Ideas Warehouse, ISBN 978-0-9548309-1-5

Why Killer Products Don't Sell,

Wiley, ISBN 978-1-906-46526-1

Thinking of.. Buying a Cloud Solution? Ask the Smart Questions,

Smart Questions, ISBN 978-0-9561556-4-1

Thinking of.. Offering a Cloud Solution? Ask the Smart Questions

Smart Questions, ISBN 978-0-9561556-1-0

Thinking of.. A Cloud App on Force.com that actually makes money? Ask the Smart Questions

Smart Questions, ISBN 978-0-9561556-5-8

A book that is currently being researched in conjunction with Heledd Straker, CIO Naked Generations

Managing the iPod generation – How can you manage them when they can't hear you?

Smarter Ideas – published in Summer 2010

Glossary

There are many terms being bandied around. Below are just some of them:

BI: Business Intelligence

BAM: Business Activity Monitoring

BPA: Business Process Analysis

BPCC: Business Process Competence Center

BPI: Business Process Improvement

BPM: Business Process Management

BPMS: Business Process Management Suites

BPMT: Business Process Management Technology

BPR: Business Process Re-engineering

BRM: Business Rules Management

BSR: Business Service Repository

CRM: Customer Relationship Management

ECM: Enterprise Content Management

ERP: Enterprise Resource Planning

CEP: Complex Event Processing

COE: Center of Excellence

DM: Document Management

KPI: Key Performance Indicator

NLP: Neuro Linguistic Programming

SLA: Service Level Agreement

SOA: Service Oriented Architecture

Notes pages